Photo by Jude Dillon

About the Author

Brian Brennan is an award-winning and best-selling author who specializes in books about the colourful personalities and social history of western Canada. His recent titles include *Romancing the Rockies: Mountaineers, Missionaries, Marilyn & More* (Fifth House, 2005), a finalist in the 2005 Banff Mountain Book Competition, and *Scoundrels and Scallywags: Characters from Alberta's Past* (Fifth House, 2002), a finalist for the 2003 Grant MacEwan Author's Award, one of the richest literary prizes in Canada. He is also the author of *Máire Bhuí Ní Laoire: A Poet of her People* (The Collins Press, 2000), which was nominated for the 2001 Irish Times Literary Prize. He was the first winner of the Dave Greber Freelance Writers Award, presented in 2004, and has made frequent appearances as a guest storyteller on CBC Radio's *Daybreak Alberta*. For more information about Brennan and his work, visit his website at www.brian-brennan.com.

Cover and interior design by Kathy Aldous-Schleindl
Cover image © Ron Watts
Interior images courtesy Patricia and Allan Gray
Edited by Kirsten Craven
Proofread by Ann Sullivan
Scans by Keith Seabrook / ABL Imaging

A Note on the Type:
The type in this book is set in Bembo with headings in Love Letter Typewriter.

The author gratefully acknowledges the financial support of the Alberta Foundation for the Arts and the Alberta Historical Resources Foundation.

Canada Council for the Arts

The publisher gratefully acknowledges the support of The Canada Council for the Arts and the Department of Canadian Heritage.

We acknowledge the financial support of the Government of Canada through the Book Publishing Industry Development Program (BPIDP) for our publishing activities.

Printed in Canada by Friesens

06 07 08 09 10 / 5 4 3 2 1

First published in the United States in 2007 by
Fitzhenry & Whiteside
121 Harvard Avenue, Suite 2
Allston, MA 02134

Library and Archives Canada Cataloguing in Publication Data

Brennan, Brian, 1943-
     How the West was written : the life and times of James H. Gray / Brian Brennan.

Includes bibliographical references and index.
ISBN-13: 978-1-894856-62-1
ISBN-10: 1-894856-62-7
     1. Gray, James H. (James Henry), 1906-1998. 2. Historians--Prairie Provinces--Biography. 3. Authors, Canadian (English)--20th century--Biography. 4. Journalists--Prairie Provinces--Biography. 5. Editors--Prairie Provinces--Biography. 6. Prairie Provinces--Biography. I. Title.

PN4913.G68B74 2006   971.2'03092   C2006-902900-8

Fifth House Ltd.
A Fitzhenry & Whiteside Company
1511, 1800-4 St. SW
Calgary, Alberta T2S 2S5
1-800-387-9776
www.fitzhenry.ca

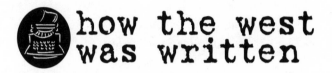

how the west was written

The Life and Times of James H. Gray

Brian Brennan

FIFTH
HOUSE

For the children of James H. Gray:
Pat, Alan, and Linda

Contents

Foreword

I met James Gray in the spring of 1995. I had just written new introductions to several of his books that were being republished and he wanted to treat me to lunch at Calgary's Petroleum Club. He was legally blind by then, and I found him holding court at the club entrance, recognizing old friends by their voices and getting caught up on the latest gossip.

Twenty years earlier, as a fresh history student embarking on graduate studies, I would have sniffed at Gray and his work for not being scholarly, not being theoretical enough. After all, academic writing was serious stuff. But, as I gradually learned during my university career, that's exactly why Gray enjoyed such a popular following. Unlike the monographs produced by most professional historians, his books were deliberately pitched at the general reader. It really was not a fair contest.

Gray turned to writing out of desperation. In a letter in December 1994, prepared on an old typewriter that had become a challenge for him to operate because of his eyesight, he confided to me, "The most important fact to be understood about me is I am a product totally of the Great Depression." He then went on to explain that in 1931, after "a five-month detour through a T.B. sanatorium," he and his young family found themselves "utterly destitute on unemployment relief, living, eating, sleeping, and cooking in a single room in a slum boarding house."

It was at this low point that Gray decided to become a

journalist. Through sheer persistence, he landed a job as a reporter with the *Winnipeg Free Press* in 1935. Soon, he was recruited as an editorial writer. But the Depression still haunted him, so in 1946, while working as a member of the Ottawa press gallery, he wrote *The Winter Years*, a personal account of the dirty thirties in the urban West.

For a number of reasons, the manuscript would not appear in print for another twenty years. But when *The Winter Years* was finally published in 1966, it was an instant national best-seller. It also marked the beginning—at age sixty when most people start to contemplate retirement—of Gray's prolific writing career. Over the next twenty-six years, he produced twelve books, many of which have become classics.

Gray's trademark was an accessible and lucid style, peppered with wit and sarcasm. In *Red Lights on the Prairies*, he quipped that if western Canadian historians were to be believed, the West had been settled by "monks, eunuchs, and vestal virgins." In a similar vein in *Men Against the Desert*, he observed, "More lies have probably been told about the weather of the Dirty Thirties than any other subject except sex; yet most of the lies could have been true."

Gray's other great strength was his ability to tell a good anecdote, to put a human face on events and issues. During the 1960s, at the same time that Gray had become a full-time writer, Canadian historians began to place greater emphasis on social history and the experience of everyday people, including those on the margins of society. Gray was already tilling this ground in his writing. Even though his books may not have been based on some new methodology, or were not heavily documented, he did the necessary primary research and then communicated his findings in clear, compelling prose.

In *How the West Was Written*, Brian Brennan skilfully examines James Gray's contribution to western Canadian history against the larger backdrop of his life, family, and career. The reader not only gains an intimate understanding of Gray—his character and personality, warts and all—but also comes to readily appreciate how and why he became one of western Canada's most successful social historians. It is an engaging biography, rich in personal detail and insight. Gray would have liked this book.

Bill Waiser, August 2006

Introduction

If life had unfolded for him as he first dreamed about it, James H. Gray would never have become a writer. He would either have gone into civil engineering because he had a talent for draftsmanship, or into accounting because he had a good head for figures. But those career possibilities evaporated in 1930 when Gray, at age twenty-four, was laid off from his job as a Winnipeg grain trader because of the Depression and forced to go on unemployment relief. Everything he had learned about surviving an upbringing blighted by poverty and alcoholism now seemed obsolete. "What were we going to do with the rest of our lives?" is how he would describe his dilemma in his book *The Winter Years*. "What skill could a man acquire that would be in demand when prosperity comes back?" He looked for an answer in the Winnipeg Public Library, where he figured everything a person needed to know about the way the world worked was probably written down in a book. The challenge for Gray was to find the right books.

Gray had read few books as a child. When unemployment relief finally became his only route to survival, he scoured the stacks of the Winnipeg Public Library to add to what little he had learned before dropping out of public school at age sixteen to support his parents and younger brothers. After reading some of the first published writings of authors such as Ernest Boyd and James T. Farrell—who later went on to achieve literary glory with such books as *Portraits, Real and Imaginary* (Boyd) and *The Young Manhood of Studs Lonigan* (Farrell)—Gray decided to become a writer. His ambition was to be published in *American Mercury* magazine—a publication noted both for featuring some of the best literary journalism published in the United States during the 1920s, and for encouraging and publishing new writers. Gray never succeeded in having an article published in *American Mercury*. He did, however, receive some encouragement from a *Mercury* editor who urged him to keep writing. One year and two hundred thousand unpublished words later, Gray sold a story to the *Winnipeg Free Press* and his career as a writer was underway.

It was indeed a remarkable career. Gray went from being a victim of the Depression to a chronicler of the 1930s, first as a freelance journalist and then as a staff writer for the *Winnipeg Free Press*. From there, he went on to become a self-proclaimed "Prairie Cassandra," first as the rabble-rousing editor of a Calgary-based farm journal and later as the editor of a Calgary oil-industry magazine. He called for protectionist price guarantees for Prairie farmers, and for limitations on American ownership of Canada's energy industry. He crusaded for the restoration of mineral rights to Alberta's agricultural landowners, and argued that Canada's natural gas should not be exported to the United States until all Canadian needs had first been met. When he left journalism in 1958 at age fifty-two, he joined Home Oil as a public relations executive to promote a Canadian pipeline project. Finally in 1966 at age sixty, he embarked on a prolific and successful twenty-five-year career as the author of a dozen well-researched, exuberantly written, and eminently readable books documenting aspects of social history—most famously, whoring and boozing—never covered before by chroniclers of the post-settlement era in western Canada.

These lively and engaging popular histories—which included such titles as *Red Lights on the Prairies*, *Booze*, *The Winter Years*, and *Men Against the Desert*—sold more than four hundred thousand copies. They put Canadian history on this country's national bestseller's lists for the first time (before the rise of Pierre Berton and

Peter C. Newman) and brought Gray three honorary doctorates: the Order of Canada, the Pierre Berton Award for distinguished achievement in popularizing Canadian history, and the honour of being appointed adjunct professor of history at the University of Calgary. Not bad for a public school dropout, as Gray used to say.

I have been drawn to James H. Gray's story for quite a number of years because I see a parallel there with the story of my own life. I, too, am an accidental writer, a journalist and latter-day chronicler of popular history—albeit a writer who did not have to escape poverty and alcoholism, survive an economic depression, or write two hundred thousand unpublished words before receiving my first paycheque. My story, unlike Gray's, comes from the sunny side of the street. I was a privileged kid raised to enjoy the urban middle-class comforts of post-war Ireland; a restless refugee from the Dublin civil service who came to Canada at age twenty-three in 1966 (the year Gray published his first book) and made a new life here, first as a migrant nightclub pianist and then as a writer for newspapers and magazines.

I fell into journalism after deciding to switch from being a wandering musician of no fixed abode to a permanent resident of one place with a beer and ham sandwich in the fridge. I was enchanted by the romance of journalism; by the idea that all you needed to become a newspaperman was a pencil, a train ticket, and boundless curiosity. The train ticket part was already becoming a thing of the past by the time I got into the newspaper business in 1968—though I did subsequently meet a columnist at the *Calgary Herald*, Ken Liddell, whose preferred mode of travel was the train. Nevertheless, the idea of getting paid to travel, meet people, and write stories still appealed to me. I took some journalism courses at a Vancouver community college, sharpened my pencil, and headed off to the *Interior News*, a weekly newspaper in Smithers, British Columbia, to start my career as a scribbler. Like Gray, I was ill prepared for the task. But I was entering the business at a time when the only qualities essential for a beginning journalist were some literary ability, a plausible manner, and the phone number of an editor willing to give you a chance to chase stories. Once inside the door, it was up to you to prove you could cover any kind of assignment and file clean copy on deadline.

Gray covered every kind of assignment during his twenty-two years as a journalist—from chronicling the story of the disgruntled relief-camp residents who trekked toward Ottawa in 1935 to reporting on the revelations of Igor Gouzenko, a former cipher clerk at the Soviet Embassy in Ottawa who defected in 1945 and told the RCMP that Soviet military intelligence was operating a spy ring in Canada. These, combined with his varied experiences as a "harvest-time stooker, an office boy in the Grain Exchange, a grain-brokerage ledger-keeper, stock-market margin clerk, some-time buyer of oil and mining stock, Model T owner, race-horse trainer and failed pool-shark" gave Gray an unorthodox yet highly effective set of credentials for a social historian.

Aside from his last book, a biography of Conservative Prime Minister R. B. Bennett that he published in 1991 at age eighty-five, Gray paid little heed to party politics in his writings. His concern was with back-fence history, with the stories of how ordinary people lived, worked, and played, while in some manner influencing the course of Canadian history. "The lives of the people in our region have been full of excitement, of interest and importance," Gray wrote in a 1976 letter to then Alberta Education Minister Julian Koziak, when the author was attempting to get more Alberta history taught in the province's schools. "Yet this has gone unnoticed where acceptance is the most vital—in the lower reaches of our educational system. In order to generate in our children an appreciation of their Canadian heritage, we first have to acquaint them with the history of their own province. Only then can they avoid the mistakes made by previous generations."

Writing the untold social history of western Canada was one of Gray's great contributions. Encouraging student interest in historical studies by sponsoring history prizes and essay contests in schools and universities was another. Those are the things for which Gray should be remembered and celebrated. I knew him only casually, and there are aspects of his cantankerous personality that likely would have annoyed me had I known him better—for example, his insistence that he was never wrong, and his penchant for using a sledgehammer to swat flies. But I will always be grateful to Gray for making Canadian history matter; for making it urgent, vital, relevant, and fashionable at a time when the American political scientist Edgar Z. Friedenberg was writing patronizingly in the *New York Review of Books* that "great events seldom occur in Canada." Friedenberg could have profited from reading Gray's *Men Against the Desert*.

Brian Brennan, August 2006

Prologue:
Canada's Highest Honour

It was rainy and cool in Ottawa with the temperature dropping to three degrees Celsius during the late afternoon of Tuesday, 8 November 1988. James H. Gray, eighty-two, snowy-haired and dapper in a black tuxedo with his white moustache neatly trimmed, sat in his grey-carpeted second-floor suite at the Chateau Laurier Hotel sipping a glass of German Riesling. It was a *Qualitatswein mit Pradikat* vintage as he had requested, and he drank it while waiting for a government shuttle bus to take him to Rideau Hall. He had spent that morning and all of the previous day at the National Archives of Canada, scrolling through the microfilmed papers of Prime Minister Richard Bedford Bennett, photocopying and taking detailed notes for a biography of the politician that would be the last major work of his writing career. Now he was about to receive the country's highest civilian honour for lifetime achievement—the Order of Canada—for the previous eleven books he had written during his prolific twenty-two-year career.

In his first book, *The Winter Years*—published in 1966 when he was sixty—Gray had written about surviving the Great Depression while living on unemployment relief in Winnipeg. He had dedicated the book to his wife, Kay, "who was so much part of the surviving," and it would have been most fitting for her to be by his side when he stepped off the shuttle bus and walked into

Government House to be invested as a member of the order. Kay, however, had been suffering from Alzheimer's disease for the previous several months, and had to be placed in a seniors' lodge just four weeks before the investiture ceremony. So instead, Gray was accompanied by his sixty-year-old daughter Pat, who also had been "part of the surviving."

As was to be expected at an event honouring Canadians "whose contributions enrich the lives of their contemporaries," Gray was in select company. Some of the honourees had played prominent roles in the 1988 Calgary Winter Olympics. They included businessman Frank King, who spearheaded Calgary's successful bid for the games; downhill skier Karen Percy, who was Canada's only double medal winner (both bronze) at the Olympics; Canadian ice dance champions Tracy Wilson and Robert McCall; and Vancouver songwriter David Foster, who composed the theme music for the games. Foster wore black tie according to the Order of Canada dress code, but also demonstrated a flash of rock 'n' roll anarchy by wearing sneakers to the ceremony. "What kind of a statement is this guy trying to make?" snorted Gray. "We are not amused."

It took about an hour for the seventy honourees to be invested. The ceremony began after they took their seats in the Rideau Hall ballroom. Governor General Jeanne Sauvé and her husband, Maurice, entered in procession with their attendants, and then stood at attention on the dais under the Waterford crystal chandelier while the band played the "Vice-Regal Salute"—a hybrid tune consisting of six bars from "God Save the Queen" and eight bars from "O Canada." (The guests had been warned beforehand that they should not start singing during the "O Canada" bit.)

The names of the honourees were called in alphabetical order. Gray's turn came after that of Laurie Graham, a veteran of Canada's national ski team with six World Cup downhill victories and three national titles to her credit. He walked up the centre aisle, stood at the foot of the dais, bowed to the sixty-six-year-old Governor

General, and paused while her secretary-general read out the citation:

> Truly a Canadian hero who loves his country fervently, his social histories of the Prairie provinces have been enormously successful in bringing to life the region's heritage and in educating a generation of young Canadians. A popular historian who is also respected by academics, he is a storyteller whose infectious enthusiasm sparkles on the pages of his books.

The badge of the order was a stylized snowflake emblazoned with a crown, a maple leaf, and the Latin motto, *Desiderantes meliorem patriam* (They desire a better country). Madame Sauvé, stylishly dressed in a black velvet skirt with matching jacket, pinned the insignia on Gray's left lapel while the official photographer snapped a picture of the white-haired pair. Gray stepped back, bowed to Madame Sauvé, half turned, bowed to Monsieur Sauvé, and proceeded to a table at the left of the dais to sign the register and accept the commemorative scroll from the aide-de camp.

After the honourees had been invested, Madame Sauvé congratulated them for their efforts to "strive for and achieve a destiny far greater than personal satisfaction or material reward." The band then played the full version of "O Canada," after which the Governor General and her husband withdrew and the recipients moved to a nearby reception room to be presented to their Excellencies. While the reception was underway, the Rideau Hall catering staff set up the ballroom for a buffet dinner featuring such delectable and exotic menu items as lobster and shrimp aspic, smoked salmon, pheasant terrine in Chambertin sauce, goose liver pâté from Périgord, fillet of Alberta beef, calf sweetbreads in Marsala wine, and a seafood medley drizzled with Nantua sauce. "It's difficult to show some restraint," commented Pat as she surveyed the pastries and other dessert offerings.

Gray and Pat remained at the party until 10:30 PM, socializing with Frank King and the other members of the Calgary contingent. "Wasn't that a great time?" said Gray afterwards as they boarded the government bus to return to their hotel. "It takes my breath away to think that I came to Alberta and made a mark of sufficient depth to come to the attention of the Order of Canada."

"Indeed," nodded Pat. "And isn't it too bad that Mom can no longer join you in sharing some of these happy experiences." Kay had been by his side when Gray launched his career as a writer fifty-seven years earlier. It seemed sad to Pat that this "most loyal of fellow travellers," as her father affectionately called Kay, could not have been there to see him receive the ultimate accolade that Canada can bestow.

Early Years
1906-1922

The Winnipeg of James H. Gray's childhood was a city divided, separated by rivers and rails into districts of rich and poor, business and residential, Anglo-Saxon and European. The central commercial core, radiating outward from the intersection of Portage Avenue and Main Street, was the banking capital of western Canada and the national headquarters of the Canadian grain marketing industry. The chic and elegant south end—below the junction of the Red and Assiniboine Rivers—was home to Winnipeg's most prosperous and politically dominant citizens, including several millionaire grain magnates who came originally from Ontario with little in their pockets. To the east lay the historic francophone community of St.-Boniface, then a separate city. The suburban west end was the neighbourhood of choice for the emerging middle class, many of them merchants and white-collar business workers who had emigrated from the British Isles. The dilapidated and cramped north end—on the far side of the Canadian Pacific Railway's locomotive shops and marshalling yards—was a kind of parallel city populated mainly by poor immigrants from central and eastern Europe. Most of these had left Old World farms behind only to find themselves living in New World squalor amid what the novelist John Marlyn has called the "mean and dirty clutter" of shantytown housing with poor sanitation and no running water.

The Winnipeg of Gray's youth was also a city of wide-open drinking. He would recall how he could walk along one six-block stretch of Main Street and "never be beyond the aroma of booze that wafted through the windows and doors of the hotels." Gray counted forty-two hotels along this strip—some with such grandiose names as "The Majestic," "Grand Central," and "The Mansion House"—and noted that all sold copious amounts of beer and whisky. So did most grocery stores and drugstores.

Gray spent his childhood years in some of the poorest sections of Winnipeg's polyglot north end, never more than a block from the hotel bars where his alcoholic father drank away what little money the family possessed. In the process the young Gray established an early rapport with the kinds of economically deprived individuals that he would later write about in his books. For the Gray family it was a life of both brutal poverty and constant uprooting. The eviction notices landed regularly on the doorstep because of the rent falling into arrears. Gray remembered one two-year period when the family moved four times. His father, debilitated by an arm lost to injury as well as a serious problem with alcohol, could never hold a job for long, and the inevitable outcome was yet another eviction. "Our first years were spent in circumstances bordering on destitution," Gray would write in *The Boy from Winnipeg*. "We moved frequently, sometimes from one house to another, sometimes into and out of unfurnished rooms."

Because of what he called this "yo-yo existence," Gray learned early on in life about the entitlements of the poor. By the time he was eight, he knew that when the bailiffs came to evict the family and seize the furniture in lieu of rent, they had to leave behind a table, a chair for every family member, a few dishes, and at least one bed. "If they were kindly bailiffs, they would stack them on the verandah while we searched for alternative accommodation," he remembered. If they were not kindly, he added sadly, the bailiffs would unceremoniously dump the Grays' possessions onto the sidewalk. He would never forget the misery and humiliation of being left to guard the few remaining sticks of his family's furniture, sitting shivering on the sidewalk in the middle of winter while his parents begged yet another landlord to take them in.

Gray's alcoholic father, Harry Gray, had lost his right arm in a 1901 railway station accident in Buffalo, New York, when he tripped and fell onto the station platform while trying to board a moving train bound for Toronto. Gray would write in *The Boy from Winnipeg* that Harry was trying to get on the train because he had just received word of his mother's death in Ontario and he wanted to attend her funeral. A check of Ontario Vital Statistics' records reveals, however, that Harry's mother had died fifteen years earlier—on 2 April 1886—which would suggest Harry was hurrying to catch the train for another reason. Regardless, he never made it home. His arm got caught under the wheels of the moving carriages and he was taken to a Buffalo hospital where a surgeon amputated the arm and part of his right shoulder.

Before the accident, Harry Gray had started to turn his life around after several years of drifting. According to family lore, he was the son of John Brown, an immigrant labourer from Gainsborough, Lincolnshire, England, who changed his name to James Gray and fled to Canada at age twenty-nine in 1854 because of a family scandal involving the theft of money from a Paris bank where his brother William worked as a teller. As a child of eight, James H. Gray heard from his Uncle George—his father's younger brother—the story of the bank robbery and "John Brown's" subsequent name change. He later wrote about it in *The Boy from Winnipeg*. But Wayne Gray, a grandson of George, has since cast doubt on the reliability of George's story. He has produced genealogical data showing that the family had been using the Gray name at least as far back as 1829, when "John Brown" was four years of age, and possibly as far back as 1801, when "Brown's" father was born. No genealogical evidence has ever been found to suggest that the James Gray who came to Canada in 1854 was once named Brown. In fact, James H. Gray would tell his son, Alan, in a 1997 interview that he searched for Browns in the Gainsborough church records during a trip to England in the late 1950s and came up blank. Yet he opted to write about the Paris bank heist anyhow, because he enjoyed a good yarn and liked the idea of having a bit of notoriety in the family history.

Immigrant James Gray and his wife, the former Rebecca Turtle of Gainsborough (James H.'s grandparents), settled with their infant son John in Holland Landing, a wooded sawmill community on the shores of Lake Simcoe, Ontario, sixty kilometres north of Toronto in the township of East Gwillimbury, and raised eight more children. James H.'s father, Harry, born in 1869, was the second youngest of their seven sons.

Harry lived in the village of Holland Landing (then with a population of 580) until he was a teenager. He acquired about four or five years of formal education at the local one-room school and then drifted from job to job until he was in his late twenties. When he arrived in Buffalo, New York, he finally found his career niche. He landed a job in a shoe store that allowed him to show off his talents as a salesman and window dresser. He won a bronze medal at the 1901 Buffalo World's Fair for one of his window displays and was about to accept a job managing a store for a shoe manufacturing company when the train accident occurred.

The accident meant that Harry could not take the new job with the shoe company. Nor could he go back to the store where he had worked previously. "Fitting shoes to the feet of women customers was no job for a one-armed man, even if he could have written well enough to make out the bills," Gray would explain in the 1997 interview with his son, Alan. "He was really a tragic figure. If he hadn't lost his arm, he was set for life as a businessman. He was a good shoe salesman, and he was good at displaying shoes. That was an art form that was recognized. But at the peak of his career he fell under a train, and that was the end of him." Harry returned to Canada and settled in the farming community of

Boissevain, Manitoba, seventy-five kilometres south of Brandon, where his younger brother George ran a butcher shop. Harry made deliveries for his brother while deciding on his next move. He met the young woman who was to become his wife when he delivered a ham to her back door.

Maria Sargent was twenty-five when thirty-five-year-old Harry Gray first came to her back door. She was the daughter of John Sargent, an Irish-American Confederate soldier from West Virginia who drifted north after the American Civil War to become a farmer in Manitoba. There he met and married a young woman from Ontario named Martha Booth. In *The Boy from Winnipeg*, Gray would write that the Booth family spent five months in 1870 travelling across the country by wagon train from Guelph, Ontario, to take up a homestead in Carman, Manitoba, eighty kilometres southwest of Winnipeg.

Maria Sargent, James H.'s mother, was born in 1879—nine years after Manitoba became a province. As was the custom for many farm girls in those days, she went to work as a domestic servant as soon as she was old enough to wash sheets, make beds, and scrub floors. She met James H.'s father, Harry, in the fall of 1904, when she was working for a Boissevain-area farmer. They married in Winnipeg on 21 July 1905. He soon acquired steady work as a timekeeper and storekeeper with the federally owned National Transcontinental Railway, which was building a line eastward from Winnipeg to Moncton, New Brunswick. That meant a move for Harry and Maria ninety-five kilometres east to the backwoods of eastern Manitoba, between the rural municipalities of Whitemouth and Rennie, just outside the western boundary of what is now Whiteshell Provincial Park. James Henry Gray, their first child, was born under a sunny sky with the temperature rising to a pleasant 72°F (22°C) at Whitemouth on 31 August 1906. His parents affectionately called him Jimmie. At the time of his birth, a charismatic politician named Wilfrid Laurier was prime minister of what was then known as the Dominion of Canada, and a tenacious Canadian boxer named Tommy Burns was the heavyweight champion of the world.

The Grays lived in the Manitoba backwoods for the six years it took National Transcontinental to build the line from Winnipeg to Dryden, Ontario. Harry did not drink during this period—for the simple reason that no bars were situated near where the Grays lived—and he managed to save a big chunk of his sixty-dollar monthly salary. However, he made up for lost time when he moved his family—which by that time included two-year-old son Walter—to Winnipeg in 1911. The crowded men-only saloons of Main Street became Harry's homes away from home. Within a year, he had blown all of the family's savings—close to two thousand dollars—on booze. To add to the family's misery, he then lost his timekeeping job at the Canadian Northern Railway's Transcona locomotive shops. He fell and broke his leg while walking home from the bar one night after a heavy drinking session, and was unable to work for several months. "We were only saved from being thrown onto the street when relatives of my mother took us in," James H. Gray would later recall. At that point, the family included a third son, Robert, born in 1912.

When Maria confronted him about his boozing, Harry acknowledged that he did have a problem with alcohol but could say only that he was "being driven to drink" without offering any convincing specifics. He pointed weakly to the fact that he had a physical handicap that limited his employment possibilities, and that there was fierce competition for jobs in Winnipeg. The population of the city had swelled from 43,000 to 121,000 between 1901 and 1911 as the city started to become the banking and grain marketing capital of the West—the self-styled "Chicago of the North." Harry felt he did not have a chance when competing for office jobs against people with English accents because British immigrants held many of the office managerial positions in Winnipeg.

To boost his employment chances, Harry embarked on a program of self-improvement that included teaching himself how to write with his left hand so he could apply for clerical jobs. The Gray kitchen became a study room every evening, with Harry, Maria, and Jimmie sitting around the table practising their writing in scribblers. Harry copied passages out of books he had borrowed from the public library. Maria, who had never been to school because it was not mandatory in Manitoba when she was a child, taught herself the basics of literacy and practised signing her name. Jimmie, who had to be kept out of school for a year when he was stricken with a form of rheumatic fever called St. Vitus's dance, tried to make up for what he was missing in grade two. Harry eventually started to get low-paying office-messenger jobs and regular paycheques. But the money rarely made it home because the banks were closed by the time he got off work and the only place where he could cash his cheque was in the bars. Harry always felt the need to buy a round for the lads after receiving the money, and one round invariably led to another.

After a few years of seeing Harry blow his paycheques in the bars, Maria decided that the bars themselves—not any inherent weakness on Harry's part—were the reason for his drinking problem. If there were no bars, she believed, there would be no problem. He had remained dry during the six years they lived in the backwoods and would be dry again if he had no access to bars. Temptation would disappear and he would bring home his wages on payday. Harry agreed with this assessment and both he and Maria became active in the ban-the-bars crusade that preceded the imposition of Prohibition in Manitoba in 1916. Also active in the movement was ten-year-old Jimmie, who would later write about the experience in such books as *The Boy from Winnipeg*, *Booze*, and *Bacchanalia Revisited*. Jimmie joined the Loyal Temperance Legion with his parents and stood on street corners handing out antiliquor pamphlets. He attended temperance rallies with his father, delivered pro-Prohibition handbills to mailboxes in his neighbourhood, and learned the words to poems with such titles as "The Lips That Touch Liquor Will Never Touch Mine." When his parents discussed the temperance messages of such writers as Edmonton suffragist Nellie McClung and Winnipeg novelist Ralph Connor (the pen name of a Presbyterian minister named Charles William Gordon), Jimmie listened intently. "By the time I was ten, I knew more about the devastating effects of booze on family life than a beer truck filled with Nellie McClungs and Ralph Connors."

After the frequent moves of the family's first years in Winnipeg, Harry discovered he could live rent-free as an apartment janitor. At that point the family's living arrangements became more stable. The rent remained free as long as Maria was prepared to regularly scrub the hallway floors and shovel coal into the furnace—something Harry, with his one arm, was incapable of doing. Moves now only occurred whenever a war veteran came home to reclaim the janitor's job he had held before the war. Sometimes this meant the Grays could relocate to a nicer neighbourhood than the one they were vacating. At one point they lived in an eight-suite apartment building in the upper-crust suburban neighbourhood of Fort Rouge, where Jimmie noted enviously that every boy in his class owned a baseball glove and a pair of hockey skates. "With a non-alcoholic father we would probably have missed both sides of the tracks, taken root on a respectable street in St. James [on the western outskirts of the city], and missed all the fun."

While "fun" might seem like an odd word to describe a life marked by alcoholism, poverty, and the trauma of being picked upon and bullied every time he moved to a new school, Gray did seem to find much to be grateful for during his first years in Winnipeg. His affectionate descriptions of hockey games played on the frozen Assiniboine River, of streets roofed with canopies of American elms, of summer picnics on the beaches of Lake Winnipeg, and of bells tinkling on the Eaton's delivery sleighs suggest that—for some of the time at least—the Winnipeg of his boyhood was indeed, as he would describe it in *The Boy from Winnipeg*, a "marvellous, exciting and wonder-filled world for small boys." He fondly recalled the tingle of excitement he felt when he and a

group of fellow ten-year-olds spent several days playing a dangerous game of hide-and-seek looking for an escaped murderer and
bank robber named Jack Krafchenko. (Fortunately for Gray and his
friends, they never tracked down the desperado.) He also had fond
memories of the time he earned more than fifty dollars at the
River Park racetrack cashing in winning tickets that the gamblers
had thrown away in ignorance because they did not understand the
intricacies of the parimutuel betting system.

When he grew older, and compared himself to the rich kids in
Fort Rouge, Gray realized just how poor he actually had been. Yet
at the same time he would recall that his poverty had been neither
restrictive nor permanent. He had been rich in expectations.
During the First World War, jobs were plentiful and lack of education was no bar to advancement for eager and industrious young
men. Gray had been able to look beyond the present to the promising future that hard work would undoubtedly bring. "Rapid
advancement was possible on ability alone," he would write in *The
Winter Years*. "The so-called professions had not yet become gov-
ernment-sheltered monopolies, and professional unions were not
yet blockading the avenues of advancement."

Gray described his father as a "periodic drunkard" who could
go for months at a stretch without taking a drink. That meant life
would sometimes take on a semblance of stability for the Grays.
During these occasional dry spells, Harry would get a job as a clerk
or night watchman, save his money, and pay off outstanding bills.
However, his family remained resigned to the fact that he could fall
off the wagon at any time. It was not until Prohibition closed the
bars in 1916 that Harry was able to stay sober continuously and
keep a job for longer than a few months. In 1917 he obtained a
low-paying clerical job with the comptroller's department at city
hall and held onto it for five years. At the end of that time, the
hotels started to reopen their bars for beer sales and the temptation
to drink again proved too strong for Harry. The result, as Gray
would write, was entirely predictable. Harry managed to hide his

problem from his city hall bosses for a few months but was eventually fired for the shameful offence of stealing from the petty cash to buy booze.

Having an alcoholic for a father was stressful for young Jimmie. He could derive some consolation from the fact that his family situation was no different from that of others he knew in the tough neighbourhoods of his youth. He could also rationalize that he should view it as "normal" for him to be growing up in an atmosphere of poverty and alcoholism. Yet the fact remained that he was continually embarrassed by a father who could not maintain a stable and secure environment for his family. Gray would later write cheerfully that the experience allowed him to "set some kind of record for school transfers" and "savour most of Winnipeg's most interesting environments." But it is clear from what he told his son, Alan, in a 1997 interview that his father's alcoholism and the taunts of neighbourhood children distressed Gray greatly at the time. Whenever he heard the kids shouting, "Hey, there's Jimmie Gray taking his old man home again," he would hang his head in shame, pretend he could not hear the taunts, and angrily push his lurching father through the front door. "It was very embarrassing to have to walk down the street with my father staggering and leaning on me," he told Alan. "But I did it for three or four years." The words to a sentimental temperance song of the period, "Father, Dear Father, Come Home With Me Now," assumed a particular poignancy for young Gray because of such episodes. He would write that he was well into his teens before he could keep from breaking down whenever he heard such lines as "the house is so lonely, the hours are so long, for poor weeping mother and me."

One of the most horrific alcohol-related incidents for Jimmie and his mother, though not, oddly enough, of lasting consequence for Harry himself, occurred on a payday night in the winter of 1913 when Harry was attacked and beaten outside a bar, robbed of his money, and left to die in the snow. He was discovered there some hours later and spent five weeks in the hospital being treated for pleuropneumonia. When he recovered he found another job and went back to the bars (though not to the one where the attack occurred) as if nothing had happened. That meant he left Maria fretting anxiously every payday if he was not home by the time she started cooking supper. She would send Jimmie down to the "corner"—in reality, the bar in the Queen's Hotel at Notre Dame and Portage Avenue—to look for Harry. If Harry happened to be in "the longest bar in the West," as the Queen's owner liked to call his place, a loud confrontation would inevitably ensue between Harry and the owner—who feared losing his liquor licence because a child had entered his bar. "Get that goddamn kid the hell out of here!" the bartender would yell. "You know that kids are not allowed in this bar."

Because Harry could never be relied upon to bring money home after cashing his cheques in the bars, Maria kept the family fed and clothed by taking whatever menial jobs she could find. In the absence of a permanent relief system for the poor, she had no other choice. She worked nights as a cleaner at the Winnipeg Electric building and took in the neighbours' laundry during the day. "She kept my father throughout his adult life," Gray remembered.

Harry's younger brother George, who changed occupations from being the town butcher in Boissevain to working as a CPR station agent at Kenton, Manitoba, eighty kilometres west of Brandon, often helped out the family with a gift of ten or fifteen dollars whenever he came into Winnipeg to do some shopping. It was a gift that usually came with strings attached in the form of a lecture from George about the stupidity of cashing one's pay-cheques in the bar. Gray would later recount a typical family conversation in *The Boy from Winnipeg*:

> "Why can't you be like everyone else, just have a beer or two, and then leave?" George would say to Harry. "Why do you always have to make a pig of yourself and not stop until

you've drunk yourself out of house and home?"

Harry would nod mutely in agreement, but he never had an answer.

"I don't know," he would say. "I just don't know. I try. God knows I try. But I don't know what happens to me. I just don't know."

At one point, Maria tried to prevent Harry from taking his cheques to the bar by having Jimmie meet him after work on payday and escort him directly home. More often than not, however, Harry would get to the bar before Jimmie arrived, and Jimmie would end up having to drag his father home drunk.

Jimmie continued to escort his father home from work even after Harry stopped drinking during Prohibition. As a result, Jimmie was able to witness events that added to his store of vivid boyhood memories and provided him with fodder for future books. One such event occurred in 1917, when the federal government decided that compulsory military service was needed to ensure that Canada had a plentiful supply of soldiers for the Great War in Europe. Jimmie and his father were attending an anticonscription rally in downtown Winnipeg when a riot broke out and soldiers were called in to restore order. As he walked away from the scene, Harry was accosted by a group of young women campaigning for the government's conscription program by pinning white roses on the coat sleeves of men they thought should join the army. One woman pinned a rose on Harry's empty right sleeve and then recoiled in horror when she realized that he was missing an arm. "She was absolutely shattered by the fact that she had put a white rose on a man who would never be eligible for the army under any circumstances," Gray would recall in the 1997 interview with his son, Alan. "She became completely flustered trying to apologize to him, but he just walked right past her. It was a very emotional moment for him, and also for me. I was embarrassed. I wanted to say something, but I didn't know what to say."

Two years later, Jimmie and Harry found themselves in the midst of another riot, when they attended an outdoor labour rally staged in conjunction with the Winnipeg General Strike—a massive labour dispute affecting more than thirty thousand workers represented by fifty-three unions. Striking city hall employees, who included Jimmie's father, forced a streetcar to stop, ordered the driver and passengers out onto the sidewalk, and then proceeded to push the vehicle over onto its side. The driver and some of the passengers responded by throwing punches at the strikers. Thirteen-year-old Jimmie had to step in to prevent his father from getting hurt. "I got him home safely before the police could arrest him."

The 1919 general strike, which Gray would describe in *The Boy from Winnipeg* as "the climacteric from which the city never fully recovered," was a pivotal event in Canadian labour history. It began in the city's metal fabricating industry over a post-war demand for better wages and working conditions, and quickly spread to other trades. It lasted for thirty-seven days, froze the economy of the city, and when it was brought to an end—with the federal government placing the city under military rule—hundreds of families saw their livelihoods destroyed. Gray would write that while the damage was greatest in families where the father lost his job and had to "remake his life in an impossible environment," the strike left his own family relatively unscathed.

Harry walked a picket line for two weeks when civic employees joined striking building and sheet metal workers in a sympathetic display of working-class solidarity. However, city council declared the sympathy strike illegal and ordered the civic employees back to work. Harry did as he was told, but he continued to support the strikers by attending their weekend rallies, and he railed constantly against the "Citizens' Committee of One Thousand" organized by Winnipeg employers to break the strike.

If it had been within his power, Harry would have stopped Jimmie from delivering the *Manitoba Free Press* during this period because the newspaper's editorial writers had denounced the strike as a communist conspiracy fomented by "alien scum" bent on establishing a Bolshevik dictatorship in Canada. However, Maria—who unlike Harry was bitterly opposed to the strike—would not hear of Jimmie giving up his paper route. The family needed Jimmie's weekly five dollars to cover the necessities that Harry with his lowly wage and Maria with her own modest income could not provide. "My income was so vital that we would have gone hungry without it," said Gray. He continued to deliver his papers even after the irate wife of a striker on his route threw a pan of soapy dishwater at him and called him a "filthy little Judas scab."

Delivering such papers as the *Manitoba Free Press*, as well as the *Winnipeg Telegram*, became Jimmie's main source of spending money from age ten onwards. Before that, starting with the outbreak of the First World War in 1914, he earned occasional money by taking to the streets to sell special extra editions of the newspapers published every few hours to give the latest news from the Western Front. However, he found it tough to compete with the more seasoned newsboys who had already staked out their positions on downtown street corners. As a result Gray took to lining his pockets instead with the proceeds from whatever he could steal and sell to local junk dealers. There was no point in asking his impoverished father to give him pocket money, so Jimmie resorted to what he called "pinching" stuff from building sites and corner stores and selling it for pennies. He kept this up until he outgrew his petty larceny tendencies, and he counted himself lucky that the police never caught him.

After leaving petty thievery behind, Jimmie threw his energies into conventional urban boyhood pursuits, such as outdoor hockey and schoolyard baseball. He also developed an interest in horse racing that brought him into direct contact with the seamier side of Winnipeg life. After several trips to the River Park racetrack, where he earned money walking overheated horses until they cooled off, he harboured notions of becoming a jockey. Older track workers encouraged him and introduced him to their adult world of fast-talking men and slow-walking women. At age thirteen, they took him to a house in the red-light district along Annabella Street—north of the Canadian Pacific Railway tracks—that operated simultaneously as a brothel and bootleg joint. When an imposing Black madam named Annie unbuttoned his shirt to give him what she called "yo' first lesson," Jimmie fled from the house and returned to the innocent world of schoolyard games and newspaper deliveries.

He continued delivering newspapers while in grades seven and eight at Alexandra Junior High. Other boys of his age were leaving school after grade eight to look for entry-level and apprenticeship positions as office clerks or carpenters. But Jimmie planned to work his way through high school and eventually parlay a talent for draftsmanship into a career in civil engineering. His belief that the key to his future lay in more education was affirmed when he scored B-class honours in the provincial grade eight exams and saw his name published—along with those of the other top students—on the front page of the *Manitoba Free Press*. However, his plans changed abruptly in 1922 when his father was fired from his city hall job for stealing the petty cash. Without seeking his parents' approval, Jimmie dropped out of Kelvin High School at age sixteen and started looking for full-time work.

Down and Out in Winnipeg
1930-1931

For the farmers of the Prairies, the economic depression that James H. Gray called "the winter years" began not with the Wall Street crash of 24 October 1929, when the free-market economy collapsed and the world's productive capacity became greater than its capacity to consume, but during the drought-prone years of the 1920s, when crops failed and farms were abandoned in parts of Alberta, Saskatchewan, and Manitoba. As for Gray and his family, their particular depression began, in effect, on 30 November 1930, when he was laid off from his job at the Winnipeg Grain Exchange and forced to go on unemployment relief.

For eight years before that, starting at age sixteen, Gray had prided himself on his ability to earn a living in what he later called "a bootstrap economy in which you learned by doing." He had dropped out of school before grade nine to help support his recently unemployed father, mother, and younger brothers Walter and Robert. His first job brought him five dollars a week for delivering groceries. From there he advanced to delivering photo engravings for seven dollars a week, and then to a job as messenger boy at the Winnipeg Grain Exchange for ten dollars a week. At that point, Gray was convinced he was "on the sure road to success." The palazzo-style Grain Exchange building, which stood ten storeys high and loomed above Lombard Avenue at Rorie Street, was synonymous with financial prosperity in post–First World War Winnipeg. The men who worked there had come west with nothing in their pockets and made their fortunes. "If they could do it, I would some day do it," Gray would write in *The Winter Years*, his autobiographical account of the Great Depression on the Prairies. "Spinning day-dreams helped take some of the sting from the cold winter evenings."

After working for a year at the grain exchange, Gray celebrated his seventeenth birthday by acquiring his first "store-boughten" suit, complete with long pants. This was an important rite of passage for Gray because, as he would write in *The Boy from Winnipeg*, "You became a man when you wore your first pair of long pants to your permanent job." He wore them onto the trading floor "with an aura of red-necked self-consciousness as my boyhood disappeared behind me without a thought, a tear of regret, or a wave of goodbye."

The Winnipeg Grain Exchange offered Gray opportunities for rapid advancement. He started by delivering telegrams for an agent representing grain-boat operators on the Great Lakes, and soon afterwards he was teaching himself office skills. He learned to type and operate an adding machine, fill out insurance policies and invoices, and grappled with the intricacies of double-entry bookkeeping. He worked fifteen-hour days, and for his efforts received a one-hundred-dollar bonus at Christmastime. "I ran all the way home clutching my envelope full of five-dollar bills."

Though his earnings at the grain exchange were rising steadily, Gray saw his job there as little more than a "temporary detour in my career." He still had his heart set on becoming a civil engineer because they "built great bridges and tunnels and made lots of money." He enrolled in an engineering course with the International Correspondence School of Glasgow, Scotland, and dreamed of the day when he would work on a project like the Grain Exchange building—"the largest office building in the entire British Empire," as he called it.

When commercial navigation ended on the Great Lakes around 1924, Gray moved in another career direction. He left the boat agent's office and moved across the hall to work as an apprentice bookkeeper for a grain options trader who encouraged him to switch correspondence courses from engineering to accounting. Promotions and pay raises followed and by the time he was nineteen, he knew the trading business inside out. He was earning $150 a month, and his annual Christmas bonus totalled $500. Only experienced bricklayers made more, he noted with satisfaction, and most bank accountants made less.

Gray's success caused him to become reckless with his money. He squandered some of it on a half interest in a couple of racehorses that never won or placed, and he lost additional money on speculative oil well ventures in Louisiana. He threw good money after bad into Colorado gold mines and Ontario silver mines, lost heavily at the pool tables, and lost additional money in the grain market. But still he clung to the belief that ultimately his gambling would pay off. He bought a late-model Ford sedan, smoked "two-for-a-quarter" cigars, and dreamed of the day when he would live in one of those "baronial" stone mansions in suburban Fort Rouge to which he had delivered newspapers as a child.

On 28 December 1926, when he was twenty and she was twenty-four, Gray took a streetcar to Winnipeg city hall and married Kathleen Margaret (Kay) Burns, an Eaton's store cashier he had been courting for a few months. She was the oldest daughter of Frank Burns, an Irish-born alcoholic who supported his wife, Ruth, and five children on the wages he earned as a janitor at the main branch of the Winnipeg post office. "By that Christmas we were so much in love that we could discover no reason for not getting married," said Gray. He could also discover no reason for giving up his gambling lifestyle—just yet. Instead of using his five-hundred-dollar Christmas bonus to take Kay on a promised honeymoon to Minneapolis, Minnesota, to buy her an imitation fur coat; buy furniture; or put a down payment on a house, he pooled resources with his employer—the grain options trader—to buy a racehorse named Dick. As a horse trainer, Gray later admitted, "I was a monumental bust." But he liked being involved in the sport of kings.

Jimmie and Kay's daughter, Alita Patricia (Pat), was born on 26 January 1928. (Jimmie chose the unusual name Alita because it was the first name of his employer's daughter.) The same year, Gray quit his job at the grain exchange and briefly went to work for a newly established firm of Winnipeg stockbrokers as a clerk, statistician, and investment advisor. His timing could not have been worse. The new business folded in December 1928, ten months before the Wall Street crash that sent a ripple effect through stock markets around the world.

Instead of immediately going back to the grain exchange, Gray decided to go into business for himself. He bought a candy-jobbing franchise and spent the first half of 1929 working eighteen hours a day restocking his dispensing machines with plastic bags that Kay had filled with mints and caramels. He went broke in that business within six months. He returned briefly to the grain exchange and then moved to the Lethbridge office of a Toronto mining brokerage firm, Solloway, Mills and Company, that seemed to offer good prospects but turned out to be running one step ahead of the law. (In 1931, the firm's principals, Isaac Solloway and Harvey Mills, would be jailed and fined for cheating their clients.) After a few months in Lethbridge, Gray retreated to the safety of Winnipeg, where, he realized later, he was lucky to still find a job at the grain exchange. The exchange was in financial trouble because dropping wheat prices and brokerage failures were causing hundreds of job losses, but Gray's former employer, the grain options trader, was able to find a low-paying clerical position for him.

The fires of entrepreneurship continued to burn in Gray's belly even after his failures as a horse trainer and candy franchiser. His next independent venture was a miniature golf business, which he hoped would net him one hundred dollars a day after he had covered the initial expenses of renting a vacant lot; installing the small obstacle course, overhead lights, and a cashier's shack; and buying clubs and balls. Kay acted as cashier during the day when Jimmie was working at the grain exchange, and he ran the business at night. His mother, Maria, looked after baby Pat when Kay was working the till. Like his other ventures, the mini-golf business went under after a few months. Gray managed to cover some of his debts when he found a buyer for the failing enterprise, but he still owed more than three hundred dollars to his creditors. Then on 30 November 1930, he was laid off from his job at the grain exchange.

Gray did not apply for unemployment relief right away. Every time he started to walk the five kilometres from his rented home at 36 Ruby Street to the city relief office at the corner of Xante Street and Elgin Avenue, he took a detour to see if there might be another job available somewhere. He canvassed every brokerage in the grain exchange building and attempted to leave application forms at department stores and at the post office. But nobody was accepting applications, much less offering jobs. After three months of trying, Gray finally accepted the fact that he had no alternative but to apply for relief. At that point all of Gray's immediate family—including his unemployed father, mother, and brothers Walter and Robert, as well as Kay and Pat—were living in the same house. They were almost out of food and fuel, and the rent was two months in arrears. "My number had come up and I was confronted with the ego-shattering discovery that there wasn't a single employer in all Winnipeg who would give me a job," Gray said in a 1996 interview with Calgary literary historian George Melnyk. "Applying for relief would prove the most humiliating experience of my life." The low point came for him one day when he had to borrow a child's wagon from a neighbour so he could haul the family sofa to a second-hand store and sell it for five dollars to buy food and fuel. "The desperation that comes to a person who is destitute is something frightful," he told Melnyk. "It's physically painful."

Gray thought his unemployment would be temporary. So did thousands of other out-of-work Prairie residents. So, for that matter, did the municipal, provincial, and federal governments, which offered unemployment relief as temporary assistance (much like employment insurance today) to tide workers over until they could find other jobs. In Winnipeg the unemployed were expected to earn this relief by working at the city lumberyard ("the Woodyard," as Gray and his fellow workers called it), sawing cordwood for use in city homes as stove fuel, or by doing other make-work projects, such as sweeping back lanes, pulling dandelions, or digging ditches. The system was simple and virtually foolproof: no work, no relief vouchers.

To obtain relief, Gray first had to stand in line for hours to fill out an application form, wait two days for an investigator to approve it, and then go down to the relief office every Tuesday to stand in line again to pick up vouchers for groceries, rent, and fuel. "This was the new world in which no cash ever passed from hand to hand." The monthly allowance for himself, Kay, and Pat was sixteen dollars for food, thirteen dollars for rent, and ten dollars' worth of cordwood for fuel. Gray's parents received a separate allowance, as did his brothers. "It was possible to live on these allowances because of the collapse in price structure." Between 1931 and 1932, the cost of a quart of milk dropped from ten cents to six cents, while the cost of bread dropped from one loaf for six cents to three loaves for a dime.

While the relief vouchers covered such essentials as food, rent, and fuel, they did not cover such incidentals as toothpaste, razor blades, or tobacco. The constant challenge for the Grays—as for all families on relief—was to find ways to earn the minimum of $1.50 a week, which they would require to treat themselves to the occasional movie or new pair of stockings. Gray thought he had a sure-fire way of earning this money by walking overheated racehorses at the track until they cooled down—just as he had done as a teenager. However, the relief office served notice that any recipient seen at the track would be cut off relief. That meant the Grays could only make extra cash by selling or pawning whatever clothing or household items they could spare. Despite their meagreness, the relief allowances did give the Grays some breathing room while they contemplated their next move. Gray's father and brothers Walter and Robert eventually decided to ride the rails to Ontario on a cattle train and look for work in the lumber and textile mills. Gray's mother stayed behind until her husband could afford to send for her. Meanwhile Gray found rooming-house accommodation that he could rent for the thirteen dollars a month allowed by the relief office. He looked forward to the spring when he felt he would surely find another job. Until then he resigned himself to sawing cordwood, sweeping back lanes, and shovelling snow on downtown sidewalks to qualify for his relief allowance.

While waiting in line for relief vouchers and participating in make-work projects occupied much of Gray's time in early 1931, he also had time for some leisure activities that did not cost him anything. He and his Woodyard colleagues spent many hours playing pickup baseball in school playgrounds and playing "dark pool" (i.e., without overhead lights) in the basement of the grain exchange building, courtesy of a friendly poolroom operator who let them use the tables as long as they did not incur any electricity expenses. Gray and Kay also spent many hours walking through Winnipeg's residential neighbourhoods looking at houses under construction: "Very few homes were being built, so it was a long walk between houses." They borrowed books on house building from the public library, and developed a body of knowledge about carpentry, masonry, and building codes that they would later put to good use when they could afford to leave rental accommodation behind and build a home of their own.

Before learning how to build houses, however, Gray first had to learn how to cut wood. His initial make-work wood-sawing assignment while on unemployment relief was a humiliating experience for him. He owned no workwear because he had never done manual labour before, and so he wore the only clothing he had for a cool day in Winnipeg: a form-fitting overcoat with a velvet collar, light chamois gloves, a soft felt hat, silk scarf, silk socks, and light oxford shoes. The foreman drew him to one side and warned him that he should be wearing proper work clothes: "Don't come around here all dressed up like a dude to buck wood." Gray replied indignantly that these *were* his work clothes: "I've been going to work all my life in clothes like these. They're the only clothes I have." The foreman insisted that the clothes were inappropriate for a labourer on a work site, and told Gray he should get the kind of safety shoes, coveralls, and gloves that the other workers were wearing. This made Gray see red. "Look, if I had money to buy work clothes with, I wouldn't be on relief," he said. "And anyway, what clothes I wear is none of your business."

Despite his humiliating experience at the Woodyard, Gray decided that sawing cordwood was actually one of the more socially useful activities listed among the relief office's mandatory make-work projects. He considered the rest of the activities–what he called "compulsory boondoggles," which included digging ditches and grading streets in parts of the city where nobody lived—to be a chronic waste of time. He felt his days would have been more productively spent knocking on doors, looking for a real job. However, he needed a doctor's certificate before he could be excused from work-gang detail. His opportunity to get one finally came in April 1931 after he had been suffering from a heavy cold for two months. After undergoing x-rays and blood tests at the Winnipeg General Hospital, the emaciated Gray ("I was five feet eleven inches tall and I weighed 118 pounds with most of my clothes on") learned he had tuberculosis in his right lung. He panicked when he heard the news: "It was spring, things had to improve, and I had to get a job. With me sick, what would happen to Kay and Patty and my mother?"

Being ill meant that Gray was temporarily unemployable, and as a result he no longer qualified for unemployment relief. Instead he now had to go on welfare, which meant dropping down to the lowest rung of society's economic ladder. This was very humiliating for someone who had once prided himself on his ability to succeed in a bootstrap economy. The local city health nurse suggested that Gray go to a sanatorium to recuperate, but he opted to remain at home in bed. This arrangement lasted only briefly, until a box of what he dismissively called "social welfare groceries" arrived at the door to keep the Gray family eating for the next month. One look at the dried peas, lentils, beans, and salted meat convinced Gray that he and the family should make other plans. His mother sold off the rest of her furniture and used the money to join her husband and Gray's brothers in Galt (now Cambridge), Ontario. Kay and Pat moved into the Winnipeg home of her parents and two unmarried sisters, while Gray got ready to spend a couple of months at the King Edward Sanatorium.

That hospital stay in 1931 would turn out to be a key turning point in Gray's life. A well-read patient named Johnny Timchuk convinced him that chasing after nonexistent jobs was a one-way ticket to nowhere and that self-education through reading was the only way to acquire the skills he would need for survival once he got off relief. "When I left the hospital, I was afire with determination to make some sense out of the world while I waited for employment to find me."

Reading and Writing
1931-1934

James H. Gray's program of self-education began in the library of Winnipeg's King Edward Sanatorium during his two-month stay in 1931 when he was recovering from tuberculosis. Fellow patient Johnny Timchuk convinced him he should take advantage of his situation to learn something about the way the world worked. "People like us, with tuberculosis or on relief, are living in Utopia," said Timchuk. He was a former dishwasher and railway cook who had spent five years in the sanatorium and had read enough books to qualify as the institution's unofficial philosopher-in-residence. "For the first time in history, people like us can stop worrying about making our own living, because society is keeping us. Think of that! It is giving us a chance only the wealthy once enjoyed— to understand the world in which we live."

Timchuk's relentless quest for knowledge profoundly affected Gray: "He passed the fever on to me, and it was not long before I was almost as hopelessly addicted to reading as he was." Never much of a serious reader before that, Gray began devouring the works of Karl Marx, Charles Darwin, the Scottish philosopher David Hume, and William Montgomery Brown—an American Episcopalian bishop defrocked in 1924 for espousing communism. Novels were not part of his reading program. Years later, Gray would tell newspaper interviewers that he had no time for fiction;

social history and current affairs were his only interests. Other Gray favourites at that time included the nineteenth-century American economist and social critic Thorstein Veblen, author of *The Theory of the Leisure Class*; the neoclassical English economist Alfred Marshall, author of *Principles of Economics*; and the English agnostic Thomas Henry Huxley, whose rejection of all things immune to scientific explanation would serve to define Gray's own ambivalence about the existence of God.

Gray continued his quest for knowledge after he left the sanatorium and resumed living on unemployment relief. His home at that point was a tiny unfurnished second-floor bedroom in a rooming house on Furby Street in Winnipeg—the best he could get for the monthly thirteen dollars allowed by the relief office. After he and Kay furnished the bedroom with beds, a dresser, a kitchen table, and chairs, there was barely enough room to move. They cooked on a small hot plate, and shared a bath and washing machine with six other families in the rooming house. Pat played in the hallway when her parents were not taking her out for walks or sleigh rides. The Grays lived like this for a couple of months until they could stand it no more.

Their next home, which they rented in a hurry, was a bedroom in a Kelvin Street rooming house with even less floor space for their furniture. They had to stack the chairs on the double bed or on the kitchen table—depending on whether they wanted to eat or sleep—and leave Pat's dismantled bed propped up against a wall in the hallway. When they ate, they sat on the edge of the double bed with the chairs piled up behind them. At bedtime they transferred the chairs from the bed to the tabletop. This unsatisfactory arrangement lasted little more than a week.

The Grays then moved to a ramshackle one-storey house on Chalmers Avenue in the Elmwood district of northeast Winnipeg. The landlady, a seventy-seven-year-old English-born widow, gave them permission to use one room for sleeping and another for cooking and eating. She also gave them the use of the yard for Pat to play in. After the claustrophobia of the Furby and Kelvin Street rooming houses, this place seemed like a palace. Its only drawbacks were a lack of insulation and proper heating, which necessitated that the Grays sleep together in the same bed and keep the stove burning past midnight throughout the winter. However, on balance, it proved to be more comfortable than any of the other homes the Grays lived in while on relief. They enjoyed spending Christmas there in 1931, especially after Kay earned fifteen dollars working as a temporary cashier at Eaton's during the seasonal rush. Gray did not report the money to the relief office. "We needed so many things so desperately that we had no conscience trouble."

The William Avenue branch of the Winnipeg Public Library became what the journalist Andrew Cohen has called a "cathedral of curiosity" for Gray once his living arrangements became more settled and he was able to continue pursuing his quest for knowledge. The library was located halfway between the Chalmers Avenue house and the relief office. Gray invariably stopped there while on his way to pick up grocery vouchers and assignment slips for compulsory work-gang detail. He read books on political and economic theory and decided that others on relief should be doing the same. Instead of being required to rake leaves or pull dandelions from city boulevards, they should be allowed to upgrade their education. Gray developed a proposal to this effect and sent it to city hall, where nobody did anything with it. "Eventually I forgot the whole project and concentrated on my own education by reading my way through the public library." As part of his self-education process, he wrote down lists of unfamiliar words, looked them up in the library dictionaries, and recited the meanings over and over as he walked home.

The public library was a haven for many unemployed Winnipeggers during this period. It offered warmth and quiet, as well as a place where they could search for a light to lead them out of the darkness of poverty and deprivation. For some that light seemed to burn in the writings of Richard Ingalese, a California mystic who claimed that the human mind could control the universe, and that success in life came to those who developed the power of absolute concentration. For others, the light seemed to burn in the monetary reform theories of the English economist John Maynard Keynes or in the untested economic concepts of Major Clifford Douglas, the English-born architect of the system of fiscal control known as "social credit." For Gray the light burned in the writings of *American Mercury* magazine founders H. L. Mencken and George Jean Nathan, whose graceful prose, satiric commentary, and hard-hitting coverage of American social and political issues inspired Gray to launch his own career as a writer.

Gray had been on unemployment relief for more than a year in 1931 when he decided to become a writer. The impetus was the providential discovery of several discarded back issues of *American Mercury* filling up a closet of one of the rooms he rented during that period. The *Mercury* was planning to run a series of investigative articles on misdemeanours in sports, and Gray decided he would try to write a piece about racehorse doping. He was not deterred by his lack of writing experience: "The libraries were full of books by the unqualified—Joseph Conrad, Mark Twain, Robert Service, Thomas Paine, Charles Dickens, Ernest Hemingway, and a hundred others. Besides, the *American Mercury* was noted for the opportunities it had provided for new and unknown writers."

His friends at the grain exchange armed Gray with a plentiful supply of notebooks, foolscap paper, and pencils as he started the research for his doping story. He investigated it thoroughly, building on the knowledge he had acquired during his teenage years as an employee at the River Park racetrack, and later as part owner of a racehorse that never won a race. He interviewed doctors and veterinarians, and gathered information from horse trainers and track workers who told him about administering shots of brandy or heroin to horses before races. He rewrote the five-thousand-word article six times before deciding it was ready for submission. He typed it out using a typewriter borrowed from the office of Sam

Drache, a friendly young Winnipeg lawyer who had helped Gray sell his failing miniature golf business in October 1930 without charging him a fee for the service.

By the time Gray's article arrived at *American Mercury*, several more issues of the magazine had been published, and the editors had chosen another article about horse racing for publication. But Gray did receive an encouraging note from *Mercury* editor Charles Angoff that convinced him he should not give up on writing just yet. Over the next year, Gray wrote close to two hundred thousand words in dozens of articles that he sent off to magazines in New York and Toronto with the hope of being published. "I never found a customer," he would later note ruefully. In his efforts to imitate the pungent critical style of H. L. Mencken, Gray developed what he later characterized as a "meat axe" style of writing that held little appeal for many American and Canadian magazine editors. But he still kept on trying to persuade them to publish his words.

While his educational upgrading and writing practice took up much of his time in 1932, Gray frequently stopped in at the grain exchange to see if there were any jobs available. He did this until he wore out the seat of his last pair of pants, after which he became self-conscious about visiting the white-collar workplace. He knew he had no chance of getting an office job while wearing a government-issue relief uniform, and so he was grateful when a former employer took pity on him and offered him one of his old suits. The suit was several sizes too large, but Gray got around this problem by persuading a friendly tailor to chalk on the alterations and then having Kay do the sewing. That suit kept him going until he and Kay were off relief. "When we thought of the dirty trick we were playing on the tailor, we agreed that when we got off relief I would go around and buy a suit from him," he would write in *The Winter Years*. "But I never did."

Another clothing crisis occurred for Gray in 1931 when he wore out the soles of his only pair of shoes and had to stick cardboard in them to protect his socks. Kay tried to help him by asking for a new pair at the home welfare office, but she was embarrassed by some female charity workers at the office who noticed she was wearing her diamond engagement ring. What, they asked, was a jewellery-clad woman doing, trying to beg a pair of shoes for her husband? They did not know, of course, that Kay and Jimmie had sold or pawned just about everything else they owned, including their car, his watch, fountain pen, cufflinks, radio, and "every bit of surplus household equipment we could spare." But they had never considered parting with her engagement ring because it had too much sentimental value for them. Upset by the taunting of the welfare-office workers, Kay returned home without the shoes, and Gray eventually solved the problem by obtaining a three-dollar workboots voucher at the relief office. He convinced an Eaton's clerk that dress oxfords were workboots for white-collar workers and bought the needed shoes. Kay spared herself future embarrassment by leaving her engagement ring at home whenever she went shopping for groceries with relief vouchers.

With his clothing needs temporarily taken care of, Gray decided to go into politics. He joined the Independent Labour Party of Manitoba (ILP)—a workers' party that hoped to capture the unemployed vote in the provincial election of 1932—and put his name forward as a candidate in the election. However, he had no talent for street-corner oratory—one of the essential qualifications for a labour politician—and so he stepped aside to let a Winnipeg labour lawyer named Marcus Hyman run in his place. Hyman won the seat and Gray went back to trying to become a published writer.

In the spring of 1933 Gray dusted off the racehorse-doping story he had tried selling to *American Mercury* and submitted it to the *Winnipeg Free Press* (formerly the *Manitoba Free Press*) for consideration. His persistence finally paid off. Features editor Frank Williams accepted the article for publication and encouraged Gray to write more. Gray would have framed the five-dollar cheque he received for the article, but after two years on relief he needed the money to buy groceries. He was thankful when the relief office supervisor told him the five dollars would not be deducted from his grocery allowance.

Gray wrote regularly for the *Free Press* after that, using the byline "James H. Gray." (The "H" stood for his middle name, Henry, but Gray would later say he adopted the initial as a mark of respect for two uncles on his mother's side, who both had first names starting with the letter "H.") Frank Williams at the *Free Press* loaned him books on writing and journalism from the newspaper's library, and cleared the way for Gray to write for the *Canadian Forum*, an influential Toronto literary and political journal that did not pay its contributors but reached an important readership. Gray discovered just how important this readership was when he wrote an article about the history of a Winnipeg war monument and received a complimentary note from none other than H. L. Mencken himself.

In the article Gray wrote about Emanuel Otto Hahn, the first-place winner of a 1925 contest to design the Winnipeg cenotaph who was rejected because the organizing committee did not want a German-born sculptor's name on a memorial honouring Canada's war dead. When they checked his background, the committee members discovered that Hahn, while raised in Toronto, had been born in Württernberg, Germany. The committee then announced a second competition with eligibility confined to "Canadian citizens born in Canada, elsewhere in the British Empire, or in any of the late allied countries." The winner of that contest, Elizabeth Wyn Wood, did possess the required Canadian credentials because she had been born in Orillia, Ontario. But she also happened to be Hahn's wife, and when the committee members discovered this they refused to award her the commission. They also rejected the person who came in second, for reasons they never made public. That left the cenotaph committee with the person who came in third—an English-born Winnipeg architect named Gilbert Parfitt—who won the commission by default and produced what Gray called "the only demonstrably fourth-rate war monument in the whole world." His article drew such a warm response from Mencken that Gray had the letter framed. "Your story of the Winnipeg uproar is magnificent," Mencken wrote. "In fact, it seems almost too good to be true."

The articles for the *Free Press* did not pay enough for Gray to support his wife and daughter. He continued to collect relief vouchers until the spring of 1934, when he finally landed a job marking the quotation board at a Winnipeg brokerage firm, Bingham and McKay, for ten dollars a week. This was almost two dollars less than what he and his family were receiving on relief each week, but Gray was so relieved to be working again that he grabbed the job without hesitation. He and Kay celebrated by purchasing a new electric stove from City Hydro that cost them five dollars down and five dollars a month on an installment plan. The stove would stand them in good stead over the next several years.

By the end of 1934, Gray's salary had risen to fifteen dollars a week, and he was juggling two new job offers. One came via Toronto lawyer John M. Godfrey, the newly appointed Ontario Securities commissioner. He had read some articles Gray wrote for *Canadian Forum* about mining stock racketeering—a subject Gray became familiar with while working at the Lethbridge office of disgraced mining broker Isaac Solloway in 1929—and he recommended to a friend at a Toronto brokerage house that Gray be hired as a fifty-dollar-a-week statistician. The other job offer came, also via Godfrey, from John Wesley Dafoe, editor-in-chief of the *Winnipeg Free Press*. Godfrey had told Dafoe that if he paid Gray's travelling expenses to Toronto, he would open up his files so that Gray could write a series of articles for the *Free Press* about mining-stock rackets. Dafoe, who was not aware of Gray's freelance contributions to the *Free Press*, asked his managing editor, George Ferguson, to check out Gray's credentials. "If this fellow can write well enough to get a tough old criminal lawyer like John Godfrey so excited, what are we doing letting him get out of Winnipeg?" asked Dafoe. Ferguson did know about Gray's freelance work because he had commissioned a few articles from him, and he suggested to Dafoe that they offer Gray twenty dollars a week to work for them as a full-time reporter.

Gray was disappointed to hear that the *Free Press* job would pay less than half of what he could earn at the Toronto brokerage house. But after struggling for a year as a freelancer he knew that a full-time writing opportunity might not present itself again for a long time. He turned down the Toronto job, gave his notice at Bingham and McKay, and went to work for Ferguson at the *Free Press.* "I made a life decision," he would recall in an interview with Calgary literary historian George Melnyk in 1996. "Being a writer with a solid backing was the best thing that could happen to a man." The *Free Press* at that point was no longer the journalistic force it had been during the First World War era, when the newspaper promoted Winnipeg as the "gateway to the West" and boasted a circulation reach that extended from Manitoba to British Columbia. But for Gray it was a foot in the door.

On to Ottawa
1935

Shortly before joining the *Winnipeg Free Press* as a reporter in 1935, James H. Gray received word that his father had died in Galt, Ontario, at age sixty-four. He did not attend the funeral. Even if he could have afforded it, he would not have gone. His memories of his father, he would recall in a 1975 letter to Wayne Gray, a grandson of his Uncle George, were "singularly unpleasant." Harry had been a "violent drunk and a wife beater, given to vomiting on his clothes and messing his pants." He had routinely stolen the money Jimmie and his brother Walter saved from their paper route collections to give to their mother for food, and he squandered it on booze. "We come from a highly undistinguished lineage," wrote Gray in his letter to Wayne Gray. He was not aware of anyone on his father's side of the family who had been successful, aside from a nephew of Harry's named Ernie Gray, who studied piano in Germany and became managing director of the Heintzman piano showroom in Toronto after trying unsuccessfully to launch a career in Canada as a concert pianist. Gray would recall visiting the Heintzman showroom shortly after he started working at the *Free Press* in 1935 and introducing himself to his cousin, who had his nameplate on the front window. "I got as cold a reception as I could possibly get. He didn't seem all that enthusiastic about making the acquaintance of any distant relative. He just had no time for me at all." Nor did Gray get a chance to make the acquaintance of Ernie's son, Wesley Gibson Gray, who likely would have impressed the author even more because he later became a respected lawyer, treasurer of the Law Society of Upper Canada, and eventually a justice of the Supreme Court of Ontario.

Once his parents and brothers moved to Ontario, it seemed that Gray wanted to have nothing further to do with them. Part of it had to do with the fact that he had never been particularly close to his brothers because "there was too much of an age difference there." He hardly ever went to visit them in Ontario and they never came to Winnipeg. As a result, Gray's children thought of their extended family as being all on Kay's side in Winnipeg. Grandma Ruth Burns was a great favourite with the Gray children, as were the three Burns aunts and the uncle, Tommy Burns. There was great sadness in the family in the fall of 1944 when Grandma Burns was killed by a streetcar when crossing the road after stepping off another streetcar near Redwood and Main. Her daughter Lillian, by sad coincidence, had been killed on 9 January 1931 at age nineteen when she was struck by a streetcar in front of the Burns home on Harbison Avenue. "Two tragedies," recalled Gray's daughter Pat. "It was just terrible."

Gray joined the *Free Press* just in time to land an assignment that he would later characterize as "the most exciting story I ever covered in my career in Canadian journalism." After six months on the night police beat—the traditional proving ground for young reporters—Gray was assigned to cover the Winnipeg leg of the 1935 "On to Ottawa Trek," a trans-Canada freight-train odyssey involving more than two thousand striking residents of federal unemployment relief camps. The army-run, relief-camp system had been established in 1932 to provide accommodation and work for single, unemployed Canadian males. The strike was a plea for dignity and respect. The disillusioned camp residents wanted an end to hopelessness and a return of meaning to their lives. They felt they had been simply dumped in these camps and then forgotten about. They also wanted more money than the twenty cents a day the government was paying them. As Gray would write in *The Winter Years*, there was something about that twenty cents a day that came to symbolize everything that was wrong with the lives of people on relief: "It affronted human dignity as little else could have done. It was just the right size to be insulting."

Things came to a head in April 1935 when fifteen hundred camp residents in the British Columbia Interior downed tools, travelled by train and truck to Vancouver, and took part in a massive sit-in at Stanley Park organized by the revolutionary Workers' Unity League—a national trade union federation backed by the Communist Party of Canada. Over the next two months, these unemployed "strikers," as the newspapers characterized them, held a series of demonstrations and tried to arrange meetings in Vancouver with municipal and provincial government officials, but nobody wanted to meet with them. At that point, one thousand of the strikers decided to take their case to Ottawa. They clambered aboard eastbound freight trains and stopped off along the way at Calgary, Medicine Hat, Swift Current, Moose Jaw, and Regina to pick up new recruits. One thousand unemployed men joined the trek as they journeyed eastward.

The strikers planned to spend four days in Winnipeg and continue adding to their numbers as they travelled across Ontario. They were operating on the false assumption that the Canadian Pacific Railway would allow them to ride all the way to Ottawa without interference. However, Prime Minister R. B. Bennett, mindful of the growing public sympathy for the strikers, had already decided the trek should end in Regina. His railways minister, Robert Manion, had sent a telegram to the CPR headquarters in Montreal saying the government wanted everything possible to be done to stop the strikers from riding the rails. The RCMP intercepted the strikers in Regina on 14 June and told them their trek was over. The strikers responded by shouting defiance at the police and vowed to continue with their trek. Prime Minister R. B.

Bennett eventually agreed to a meeting in Ottawa with the trek leaders. The two thousand other strikers squatted at the Regina Exhibition Grounds—with food and tents supplied by townspeople and the Saskatchewan government—and waited for their leaders to report back.

News of the RCMP action in Regina precipitated a series of strikers' parades and mass meetings in Winnipeg, many of them organized by local communists. When the Ottawa talks broke down—with trek leader Arthur "Slim" Evans loudly denouncing Prime Minister Bennett as a liar—one of the biggest rallies ever staged in Winnipeg up to that point was held on the grounds of the Manitoba legislative building. The strikers' main demand was that they be centrally billeted by the local authorities rather than scattered in rooming houses around the city.

Five days after the rally, the strikers occupied the provincial government's soup kitchen in Winnipeg. Gray, who had "taken about all the relief camp oratory I could absorb" when he was covering the strikers' meetings, found himself at the centre of the action when the soup kitchen was seized. The strikers granted him entry, seemingly because they thought he was one of them. When they discovered he was a reporter, they briefly threatened to keep him as a hostage along with six city policemen they were holding. But Gray managed to slip away while the strikers argued over what to do with him.

The soup kitchen occupation ended peacefully when the city agreed to billet the strikers in tents on the Winnipeg Exhibition Grounds and made arrangements for the leaders to discuss other grievances with Manitoba Premier John Bracken. The focus then shifted to Regina, where strikers were holding a peaceful Dominion Day rally. The RCMP moved in with batons swinging, arrested Slim Evans and other trek leaders, and sparked one of the bloodiest riots in twentieth-century Canadian history. The riot left two dead (not one, as was frequently reported before new evidence was uncovered in 1999 by University of Saskatchewan historian

Bill Waiser), hundreds shot or otherwise wounded, and one hundred rioters arrested.

The Regina riot ended the "On to Ottawa Trek" as far as many of the strikers were concerned. Most accepted train tickets from the Saskatchewan government and returned to the relief camps (which the strikers called "slave" camps) they had abandoned in Saskatchewan, Alberta, and British Columbia. In Winnipeg, however, the strikers continued to hold rallies while preparing to launch their own march on Ottawa. They solicited donations and raised enough money to charter nine buses to take 250 of them to Kenora, Ontario, where they hoped to board a freight train bound for Ottawa.

Gray described the journey to Kenora, which took place two weeks after the Regina riot, as "an anticlimax, almost a fiasco." When the buses reached the Manitoba-Ontario border, they were stopped by provincial police and refused permission to advance any further. Faced with the choice of returning to Winnipeg or walking fifty kilometres along a mosquito-plagued highway into Kenora, most of the strikers chose to walk. The police warned motorists that they would seize the cars of any sympathizers who dared to pick up the strikers while they were walking.

Gray travelled by train to Kenora to cover the activities of the strikers. There was not much to cover. The police constantly patrolled the CPR property to keep the strikers away from the railway lines, which left the strikers with nothing to do but hang around in city parks while their leaders decided how they should continue on to Ottawa. Gray noticed that three of the leaders, Bill Ross, Harry Binder, and Mitchi Sago, were recent graduates of the Young Communist League, which led him to conclude that their followers were not really relief camp workers at all, but a group of North Winnipeg radicals "playing at making a revolution." As a result, he was now covering what he believed amounted to a phony story. The strikers who seized the Winnipeg soup kitchen had been genuine relief camp residents, clearly identifiable by their khaki uniforms and army-surplus boots. But these Kenora "strikers" were merely rehearsing for the day when they would march on the seat of power and seize control.

Public sympathy for the visitors quickly turned to resentment when it was rumoured that they might remain stuck in Kenora for several weeks instead of leaving town within a few days. It was the height of the tourist season in Kenora, and a lengthy stay by loitering radicals was not viewed as good for business. Gray spent his time shuttling between the police station and the church basement where the visitors were billeted, but nobody could tell him what the strikers' next move would be. In a desperate attempt to kick some life into what was quickly degenerating into a non-story, Gray resorted to writing speculative pieces about what might happen if the radicals were to leave town in small groups with the intention of hopping a freight train or riding on a passenger train without tickets. However, most of what he wrote never appeared in the *Free Press*. The editors wanted news, not conjecture. After three days of no news, an end to the story was quickly written when the radicals surrendered and accepted a government offer of train transportation back to Winnipeg. Two years later, the story acquired a bizarre McCarthyite postscript when Gray was falsely accused of being a communist sympathizer.

The accusation occurred when Gray was assigned to write a series of stories about a thirty-five-year-old Ukrainian immigrant named John Hladun. He had cancelled his membership in the Communist Party of Canada after a trip to Russia convinced him that the Stalinists were bent on stamping out all vestiges of Ukrainian nationalism in the Soviet Union and moving the peasants to Siberia. When he returned to Canada, Hladun joined forces with a group of anticommunist Ukrainians in North Winnipeg who helped him get a job as a labourer in a packing plant. Gray spent the better part of a month conducting interviews with Hladun, who had been recruited into the Communist Party of Canada in his early twenties because of his involvement with the

Winnipeg branch of the Ukrainian Labour-Farmer Temple Association—a cooperative organization that owned community halls in Ukrainian settlements throughout the Prairies. Hladun had immersed himself in communist propaganda at a training school in Lockport, Manitoba, studied the works of Karl Marx and Friedrich Engels, and had been sent to the V. I. Lenin Institute in Moscow for additional training. When he went to the *Free Press* building for the interviews with Gray, he carried three notebooks filled with information about a movement to start a communist revolution in Canada and details of his own involvement in the movement.

Hladun asked that his identity be disguised in Gray's stories because he feared being killed by his former comrades. Gray found it hard to believe that Canadian communists would want to murder one of their own dropouts. But he agreed nevertheless to include enough misleading information in the stories to direct suspicions away from Hladun. The Hladun stories were set in type in the *Free Press* composing room, and packaged for syndication to newspapers across Canada. Before they could be distributed, however, Gray received a call to meet with Jim Litterick, a Communist Party member of the Manitoba legislature who had won his seat in the provincial election of 1936. Gray was shocked to discover that Litterick already had copies of the yet-to-be-published Hladun stories. "How could this have happened?" Gray wondered. "I had not yet seen the copy myself, and here was Litterick with one in the Communist Party office."

While Gray was trying to figure out who might have leaked the package to the Communist Party—"somebody in the composing room, a janitor, maybe a delivery-room employee?"—Litterick held up the stories and quietly asked, "What we want to know from you, Jimmie, is who is this guy?" Gray was unnerved by Litterick's question but feigned surprise and said he knew nothing about the articles. "Look, Jimmie, we're not going to play games here," said Litterick. "We know all about this except this man's name. That's all we want from you. We know that he used to come into the newspaper office every night and talk to you about it. And you wrote the articles, and then you consulted with him, and for the last six weeks you have been working on this thing. So don't play games with us."

Gray was now in a panic. He began to fear for his safety when two of Litterick's henchmen stood up to block the doorway, but still he refused to identify Hladun. He grabbed a heavy glass inkstand from Litterick's desk and said that if he was not allowed to leave, "I'm going to fire this inkwell through that window and start yelling my head off."

Litterick smiled and signalled to his men to step away from the door. "Jimmie, we wouldn't think of touching you," he said. "But please leave the inkwell there before you go. And there's something here I would like you to read." He reached into his desk drawer and pulled out a piece of notepaper. It contained an unsigned memo, dated July 1935, addressed to the Central Committee of the Communist Party of Canada:

> Special mention should be made of the work of Comrade Jim Gray, who is now employed as a reporter by the *Winnipeg Free Press*. He was able to obtain much valuable information about the plans of the Ontario Provincial Police and the Kenora police to attack us if our work went on. As a result of this information we were able to change our strategy to prevent these attacks. Comrade Gray is to be highly commended for his initiative in this regard.

"Walk through that door if you like," Litterick told Gray. "And when you do, let me tell you that a copy of this memo is going to the Mounties, and a copy to the publisher of the *Free Press*." Gray refused to be cowed by this blackmail threat. He went back to the *Free Press* newsroom and told the whole story—including the part about the incriminating memo—to the city editor, Howard Wolfe.

Gray thought his job might be on the line for allegedly spying on the Kenora police and feeding information to the communists, but he did not have to worry. His editor was more interested in finding out who had leaked the Hladun stories to Litterick, and in having the *Free Press* police reporters check to see if Hladun was in danger. Gray never discovered the identity of the mole at the *Free Press*. Nor did he ever hear of any harm coming to Hladun, who eventually moved to Toronto and landed a job writing for a Ukrainian-language anticommunist magazine. And if the incriminating memo ever found its way onto the desk of the *Free Press* publisher, Victor Sifton, Gray never got to hear about it.

From talking to his RCMP contacts, Gray got the impression that the Mounties probably did receive the memo, and that they responded simply by opening a file and adding his name to their list of possible subversives. The police clearly did not view him as a threat because they never questioned him about his alleged ties to communists. But Gray still had to wonder why Litterick and his associates had gone to the trouble of concocting a phony memo to blackmail him into identifying Hladun. "It always seemed to me a bit incongruous," he wrote in *Troublemaker!*, a personal history of his career as a journalist, "that conspirators who could devise a successful scheme to steal the secrets of the atomic bomb could be capable of such an act of petty meanness."

Playing Oliver Twist
1937

Canadian newspaper journalism in the 1930s was defined to a great extent by the power and influence of its top editors. Words such as "crusading" and "legendary" were used to describe such editorial titans of the period as John W. Dafoe at the *Winnipeg Free Press*, Peter Galbraith at the *Calgary Herald*, and Grattan O'Leary at the *Ottawa Journal*. They told the truth when it was not popular or profitable to do so and stood up to governments, such as the Social Credit administration in Alberta, that tried to muzzle or control them. However, as James H. Gray and a fellow reporter named John Sweeney discovered during salary negotiations with *Free Press* publisher Victor Sifton in 1937, the real power still belonged to the newspaper owners. The editors might have held sway on the editorial pages and held positions of great influence in political and business circles, but they always had to defer in the first instance to the men who controlled the newspaper purse strings.

Gray and Sweeney became the appointed spokesmen for the *Free Press* newsroom staff when the staff decided in 1937 that a 10-percent wage cut imposed in 1931 should be revoked. The economic climate in Winnipeg had improved during the intervening six years, they said, and the *Free Press* had grown sufficiently profitable for it to be able to afford the requested increase. Management did not recognize Gray and Sweeney as an official negotiating team. The *Free Press* newsroom was not unionized, so the company was under no legal obligation to engage in collective bargaining. But management did agree to meet periodically with staff to address employee concerns, and it was within this context that Gray and Sweeney made their request.

Gray, who had received twenty dollars a week when he started at the *Free Press* in 1935, and had since seen his salary rise to twenty-five dollars a week, was a reluctant participant in the negotiations. In 1937 he felt lucky to have a job—especially a writing job—and he did not want to jeopardize it by becoming caught up in a long-standing grievance by his colleagues. "I was on unemployment relief when the 1931 cut was made," he would explain in *Troublemaker!* "So how could I argue for restoration of a pay cut I had never suffered?" He relented when his colleagues said he would be working for the greater good of the newsroom. They pointed out that the newspaper's printers were being paid forty dollars a week, and told him that newsroom staffers should be similarly compensated. Sweeney, a veteran reporter, was ready to make this argument and the newsroom staffers urged Gray to support him.

Sweeney and Gray began by taking their case to the managing editor, George Ferguson, with the hope that he would relay the request to Sifton. Ferguson told them, however, that they were "in the wrong church," and said they should approach Sifton directly. He also told them they should improve their presentation:

> Go off in a corner and practise your speeches. Get your arguments down pat because you are all over the yard like a deconstipated cow. The hell with generalities about the economy. Get the case down to nuts and bolts. It probably won't drag any money out of Victor [Sifton], but you'll sound a helluva lot better doing it.

Though they were reluctant to deal with Sifton directly—he

was an austere businessman and war veteran who had lost an eye in the First World War and had a reputation for toughness—Sweeney and Gray took Ferguson's advice and developed an economic argument based on the fact that the *Free Press* was carrying more advertising in 1937 than it had in 1931 when the pay cut was instituted. In 1931, the paper had been publishing twenty-page editions every day. Now, the paper was publishing twenty-eight pages daily during the week and up to forty-four pages on Saturdays. If Sifton felt the printers were worth forty dollars a week, the two newsroom negotiators argued, "it was in his interest to pay us more money."

Sifton, the youngest son of lawyer, businessman, and politician Sir Clifford Sifton who had bought the *Free Press* in 1898, received the negotiators cordially. He listened politely while Sweeney and Gray presented the advertising figures and pleaded for the reporters to be treated with dignity and respect. "We told him that we represented the *Free Press* wherever we went," Gray would write in *Troublemaker!* "We had no identity of our own in many cases; we were 'the *Free Press* reporter' to the citizens, politicians, businessmen, and community leaders with whom we came in daily contact. At the very least we should be paid enough to be able to meet the public on common ground."

Sifton congratulated Sweeney and Gray on their presentation and said he would get back to them in a couple of days. "This is not at all as simple as it may look to you," he told them. "I'll get out our editorial budget and see how it relates to the mechanical and business departments. I've got a couple of ideas I'd like to test out. Let me do that, and we'll talk some more and see what we can work out." When Sifton met with them two days later, he dropped a bombshell. He started by acknowledging that the best people at the *Free Press* were being inadequately compensated compared to those who contributed less. But he could not revoke the pay cut of 1931 because it had served only to bring *Free Press* salaries into line with those paid for similar work in Winnipeg, and "so far as I can learn, our wages are still in line or even somewhat higher than the city average." Nor did he think it would be fair for him to give the newsroom staffers a general pay raise without increasing the wages of employees working in the advertising, circulation, and other departments. However, he could see his way toward giving selective pay raises to deserving newsroom individuals as long as they were comfortable with him forcibly retiring some older, non-productive employees and using the savings from their salaries to cover the increases.

"I was too shattered to speak," Gray would later write. "He had put the responsibility for firing the paper's longest-serving employees, with little more than the clothes on their backs to show for more than thirty years' service, right on the ends of our noses." Gray and Sweeney took their leave, returned to the newsroom, and decided that Sifton's proposal was unacceptable. They recalled the consternation Sifton had caused the previous December when he cancelled the newsroom's annual Christmas bonus and replaced it with a company pension plan that would allow employees to retire at age sixty. This latest proposal was clearly part of Sifton's grand scheme to get rid of all employees aged sixty and older. Gray and Sweeney told managing editor Ferguson that they would not be responding to Sifton's proposal, and "thus ended our labour-negotiating careers."

As it turned out, the jobs of the older staffers remained secure until, as Gray would write, "the infirmities of age forced their retirement." And while Gray was inclined at the time to denounce Sifton for his callous attitude toward aging employees, he realized afterwards that the publisher was probably no different from most other Canadian employers of that period. "Noblesse oblige imposed but a single responsibility upon them: to safeguard the solvency of the enterprise by maintaining its profitability." In fact, Sifton might even have been seen as one of the more progressive employers because he had introduced a pension plan at a time when most private companies did not have them.

Gray realized, too, that he and his colleagues had mistakenly regarded the *Free Press* as an oasis in the desert of capitalism; as a public trust with a conscience and a higher purpose. As he wrote in *Troublemaker!*, he never thought of the paper as being a business enterprise:

> The *Free Press* was us. We were the *Free Press* even to the point where, when covering assignments, we introduced ourselves [as] simply, "*Free Press*," and got around to our own names later if it seemed necessary. Our loyalty to the paper was so deep as to be almost pathological, for when we were covering an assignment we lost all sense of time. If covering a story meant working ten to fifteen hours a day for days on end, we worked those hours and regarded it as an affront to our ability to be spelled off by another reporter. The idea of asking for compensatory time off was as foreign to our makeup as was the concept of working a forty-hour week. There was, moreover, a magnet in the fourth-floor newsroom that drew us to it whenever we got within a dozen blocks of the building. Few of us ever completed a night at a concert or a movie without "dropping in to see what was doing," on the off chance we could become involved in whatever it was.

Before the meeting with Sifton, Gray and his newsroom colleagues had thought of their association with the newspaper business as a lifetime commitment. They dressed like characters out of *The Front Page*—Gray, with his slim build, tightly trimmed moustache, and fedora, looked like a young version of American billionaire Howard Hughes. He and his colleagues played the role of newspaperman as if they had been "called" to journalism in the same way that clergy are called to the ministry. "The strength of that religious commitment to the *Free Press* was never the same after our experience with Victor Sifton in the spring of 1937."

Sitting Out the
Second World War
1939-1945

For many young men, especially those who were single and unemployed, the Second World War came as a welcome break after the miseries of the Great Depression. Their world of hopeless stagnation was suddenly transformed into a world of military opportunities. They could join the army and see Paris, join the navy and see the rest of the world, or join the air force and pick up job skills that would stand them in good stead after the war. For James H. Gray, aged thirty-three when the war broke out and married with an eleven-year-old daughter, the war brought a dilemma. He was about to move his family from their one-bedroom upstairs apartment on Winnipeg's Talbot Avenue after negotiating a $3,600 mortgage to build a three-bedroom home on Glenwood Crescent, located along the flood plain of the Red River northeast of the city centre. Jimmie and Kay planned to build the house themselves, without a general contractor, using the knowledge they had acquired from library books borrowed while he was on unemployment relief. Would it be fair of him to subject Kay and daughter Pat to financial hardship by making them live on an army private's salary that would leave only twenty-five dollars a month for food and other necessities after the thirty-dollar house payments were deducted? Economics clashed with patriotism in Gray's mind.

If the war had broken out a few years earlier, or had involved circumstances other than the desire of a tyrannical dictator to rule the world, Gray might have found himself participating in antiwar protests. His father had been adamantly opposed to the First World War, and as a teenager Gray had been strongly influenced by the pacifist arguments that abounded in Winnipeg after the war. But now he was influenced by the pro-war editorials of the *Winnipeg Free Press*, which declared that Hitler would soon take over the world if people with guns did not stop him.

His economic argument for not enlisting began to weaken when Gray talked to a recruiting officer for the Queen's Own Cameron Highlanders militia unit. He discovered that if he took a commission as a lieutenant, his officer's salary would amount to more than three times a private's salary. That meant Kay would receive $135 a month to take care of household expenses for herself and Pat, while his own living expenses would be covered by the army. But the idea of parachuting into a cushy officer's job offended Gray's sense of bootstrap propriety. He weighed the pros and cons for a few months before reluctantly deciding to go the commission route.

He could have spared himself the mental anguish. An army medical examination revealed that his 1931 bout with tuberculosis had rendered him physically unfit for active service. "Get the hell out of here and don't come back," said the doctor. Gray returned home relieved, but spent the rest of the war years thinking he had "chickened out." He spent the first part of the war covering local news stories. He tried to get an overseas posting as a war correspondent but lost out to more experienced *Free Press* reporters. He did like covering events of local importance, however, especially when he became the paper's city hall reporter. "I considered it the best job, the one I liked the most, because the city council was forever dealing with problems that affected people, and you could see the reaction to the decisions they were making," he would recall in a 1976 interview with Calgary historian David Bercuson. "When

Ottawa made a decision, or the provincial government made a decision, it had to get filtered down through a whole massive kind of bureaucracy before you saw any result. But when the city streets were in a mess, and the city engineer was given instructions to fix the streets, you could see the streets being fixed."

In 1941, Gray was transferred from the city hall beat to the *Free Press* editorial board, where his job was to write unbylined opinion pieces on topical issues—articulating the newspaper's official position on the important matters of the day. This was a coveted promotion for Gray. He was no longer working in the noisy, open-area, cattle-pen atmosphere of the newsroom with its constantly ringing phones and clattering Underwood typewriters. He was now part of the newspaper's brain trust, with his own semi-private office and a ten-dollar salary boost that brought his weekly wage to fifty dollars. He bought himself a blue pinstriped suit to signify his newly elevated status, and looked forward to rubbing shoulders daily with the editor-in-chief, John Wesley Dafoe. Gray also looked forward to soaking up what he called the "intellectual ferment" generated by his fellow editorial writers. During his six years as a reporter, he had gradually come to realize that his forte was in the world of ideas, not in the world of embalming the public utterances of local politicians and police chiefs. He felt he was more temperamentally suited to participating in the discussions from which public policy sprang, rather than reporting on the events that the policies produced.

Dafoe and Gray made strange bedfellows. Dafoe, a great admirer of Sir Wilfrid Laurier, viewed the Liberals as the only party fit to govern Canada, and he promoted world free trade as the cure for all economic ills. Gray, a fan of former Conservative Prime Minister R. B. Bennett, felt the government should play a significant role in the economy through price stabilization, subsidies, grants, and public works programs. With such differing views on economic matters, it seemed inevitable that Dafoe and Gray would eventually find themselves butting heads. However, as long as there was a war on, they had more pressing concerns to write about. As Gray would write in *Troublemaker!*, every time he put paper in his typewriter he was expected to ask himself the question, "Does what I am saying advance the war effort?" In times of war, Canadian newspapers were expected to become propaganda arms of the government. They could not be antiwar advocates. If they felt the need to criticize, they could only admonish the govern-ment for certain decisions made during the course of the war; they could never quarrel with the government's decision to go to war in the first instance.

For Gray, editorial writing was "the high heaven to which all journalists must aspire." There was plenty of time for reading, and plenty of time for reflective writing without the pressure of dead-lines. Late-afternoon and evening reporting assignments were no more. The Gray family dog, a fox terrier named Perky, stopped treating its master like a stranger. Kay could now make dinner plans with reasonable certainty that her husband would always be home before 6:00 PM.

While the war effort coloured much of his thinking and informed the content of his editorials, Gray also had an opportu-nity during this period to develop some of the ideas about west-ern Canada's place in the federal system that he would articulate in future books and newspaper articles. He was particularly influ-enced by the 1940 report of the Royal Commission on Dominion-Provincial Relations—referred to in the newspapers as the "Rowell-Sirois Report" because the chairmen were Newton Wesley Rowell and Joseph Sirois. The report called for massive intervention in the economy by the federal government through transfer payments to the provinces to help provide a national min-imum level of social, medical, and educational services. The exist-ing Liberal doctrine of laissez-faire would never serve to improve the lot of the western have-not provinces, Gray concluded, "because the country was organized to destroy the economy of western Canada under that doctrine." What the West needed was a rebirth in a newly revised federal system that acknowledged the existence of regional disparities. However, Gray did not expect Dafoe, the champion of laissez-faire, to espouse this viewpoint, so he kept his political opinions to himself and concentrated on writing about local and war-related matters.

With war raging overseas, serenity prevailed on the Gray home front. The Grays' second child, son Alan Gary, finally arrived on 7 September 1940 after Kay had undergone several miscarriages. Daughter Linda Ann was born on 17 January 1942. In 1941, Jimmie and Kay sold the three-bedroom house, which they had built in 1939 for $3,600, for $5,700. A professional contractor was so impressed with the plans Gray had drawn up for the house (using skills he acquired while studying civil engineering by correspondence as a teenager) that he bought the blueprints for fifty dollars. After selling their house, Gray then built an identical three-bedroom house five blocks up the street at 134 Glenwood Crescent, and was able to take enough time off work to supervise the subcontractors almost daily. "Nobody ran herd on the time *Free Press* editorial writers spent at their desks," he would write in *Troublemaker!*

Wartime rationing, with colour-coded coupons issued for the purchase of such staples as sugar, eggs, and meat, brought many challenges in terms of balancing the family budget. For Kay, grocery shopping became almost a full-time job. Like other Winnipeg shoppers, she had to bring computer-like skills to the task of figuring out how to use coupons to buy fixed amounts of a commodity when the value of the coupons kept changing weekly. A coupon that bought 220 grams of butter one week would buy only 200 grams the next week. The government tried to make life a little easier for harried shoppers by issuing pressed-paper disks to make up the difference between the value of the ration coupons and the value of the items being purchased. But the shoppers now had to remember that the disks, like the coupons themselves, were more valuable than money. Just how valuable they were was made clear to Gray after meat rationing was introduced in 1943. He arrived home from work one afternoon to discover his two youngest children, Alan and Linda, spreading peanut butter and jelly on Kay's meat-ration disks and feeding them to Perky the fox terrier. "With the disks went the roast for our Sunday dinner," he would write in *Troublemaker!* "When none of the neighbours had any spare meat-ration disks we could borrow, Kay had to settle for beefsteak and kidney pie, with heavy emphasis on unrationed kidney and light on the stewing meat masquerading as steak."

Gray spent five years writing editorials for the *Free Press* and never produced anything during that time that he considered of lasting significance. The big issues of the day were always handled by Dafoe, the managing editor, George Ferguson, and a few other editorial-board heavyweights who considered themselves the custodians of unchanging human truth. But Gray did write one editorial calling for the future implementation of a number of post-war government initiatives—including job creation plans, better medical care, and improved old-age pensions—which earned Dafoe's approval. After being on relief during the Depression, Gray had come to believe that Canada needed a "more sensible kind of social structure" with a strong central government leading the way to ensure an equalization of social services across the country. He was wholeheartedly in favour of all programs that made life better for Canadians.

Gray was surprised that Dafoe approved of his editorial on post-war initiatives because he had always seen the editor-in-chief as an opponent of government social programs. But he discovered that, in fact, Dafoe was all in favour of social programs, as long as they were promoted by the right political party: "With Dafoe, ideas were purified or contaminated by the company they [kept]. Thus, the idea of nation-wide unemployment insurance was anathema when it was part of [Conservative Prime Minister R. B.] Bennett's New Deal [economic reform program], but something to embrace enthusiastically when the Liberals adopted it at the outset of the war."

In early 1943, Gray took a break from editorial writing to spend a month in Ottawa watching Parliament in action. Ferguson had decided that Gray should learn more about the way the government worked to add strength and authority to his editorials. Gray travelled to Ottawa with high hopes and returned home disappointed. He discovered that the important business of government was conducted behind closed doors, not on the floor of the House of Commons, and that only privileged journalists had access to the inner workings. Gray had no political contacts to tell him what was happening behind the scenes, so the stories he produced were little more than rewrites of government press releases, devoid of insight or context. He spent most of his time in Ottawa wishing he were back in Winnipeg. But he did take time out to write a freelance article for *Maclean's* magazine about a planned iron ore project in western Ontario, and that led to a job offer as the magazine's Ottawa correspondent at one hundred dollars a week—double his *Free Press* salary—plus expenses.

Gray turned down the *Maclean's* job. His brief Parliamentary Press Gallery experience had been more than enough for him. "I was repelled by the town itself, by the parliamentary charade, and by the monstrous size of the government apparatus one was expected to cover." But when he mentioned to Ferguson that he had rejected the offer, the managing editor exploded and told him he should get his head examined. "You and I know it will be years before Victor [Sifton] would ever part with that kind of money for you," Ferguson said. "For heaven's sake, don't you ever think of your family? When Kay hears of this, I hope she cuts your damn throat."

Fortunately, Kay was spared that grisly task. Sifton, as it turned out, was quite prepared to match the *Maclean's* offer. But he would only do so if Gray became the *Free Press*'s parliamentary correspondent in Ottawa, and that position was already filled. So instead Sifton agreed to pay Gray an extra thirty dollars a week to produce commentary columns about politics, as well as writing his usual quota of editorials for the paper. That meant Gray had to take occasional fact-finding trips to Ottawa and Washington to bring himself up to speed on current political developments. Gray did this for the remainder of the war years, until a change in editorial-board leadership at the *Free Press* made him revise his opinion about Ottawa and start thinking seriously about moving permanently to the national capital.

Ottawa Correspondent
1946-1947

The death of the editor-in-chief, John Wesley Dafoe, on 9 January 1944 at age seventy-seven, left the *Winnipeg Free Press* editorial board in a state of flux. Dafoe had ruled the paper for forty-three years, and as a well-connected Liberal supporter, he had made the *Free Press* one of the best-informed newspapers in Canada during periods of Liberal government. It was widely expected at the *Free Press* that his successor would be fellow Liberal George Ferguson, the managing editor who had hired James H. Gray in 1935 and who functioned as Dafoe's senior editorial writer and alter ego for more than a decade. Instead, publisher Victor Sifton—who had always resented the fact that Winnipeggers called the *Free Press* "Mr. Dafoe's paper"—gave the editor-in-chief's job to a troika consisting of Ferguson, Bruce Hutchison, and Grant Dexter.

Hutchison was a national affairs columnist for the *Free Press* who lived in Victoria, British Columbia, and did not want to move to Winnipeg. Dexter was the paper's senior parliamentary correspondent in Ottawa. He did not want to move to Winnipeg either. But the job required that the editor-in-chief be located in Winnipeg, and so Hutchison and Dexter took turns at staying there temporarily whenever Ferguson had to attend to newspaper duties elsewhere. The triumvirate arrangement seemed odd to Gray at the time because he thought it would have been simpler and cleaner for Sifton to appoint one individual—specifically, Ferguson—to succeed Dafoe. It was only years afterwards that Gray realized Sifton never intended to appoint a successor because he wanted to be his own editor-in-chief. Sifton felt he had lived in Dafoe's shadow far too long. Now he wanted the *Free Press* to be known as "Mr. Sifton's paper." He was reclaiming his birthright as the paper's most important personage. No high-profile editor would ever take that away from him again.

The triumvirate arrangement worked well for Gray when Ferguson was in charge because they had served together on the editorial board for three years and they knew and understood one another's editorial prejudices. Gray also got along well with Hutchison, who shared Gray's enthusiasm for lightening the tone of the paper with offbeat writing. Hutchison particularly liked the way Gray balanced the commentaries on national and international issues with editorials about life on the Prairies. "Without Jimmie's writing and editing skills, I would have been lost," Hutchison wrote in his autobiography, *The Far Side of the Street.* "We became fast friends and managed, often by the skin of our teeth, to fill the daily vacuum."

Dexter, however, was a different kettle of fish. He did not care about local issues and insisted that Gray and his colleagues write only about federal politics, international trade, and other issues that interested him. Not only that, but he expected the editorial writers to express the same opinions Dexter would have expressed if he had written the editorials himself. "After functioning under the Dafoe-Ferguson system of freewheeling licence to work out my own ideas in my own way, I found that intolerable," Gray wrote in *Troublemaker!* When it became evident that Dexter would be relocating permanently to Winnipeg in 1946, Gray decided there was no longer any future for himself at the *Free Press* and began to think seriously about getting out.

Ferguson, who was already planning his own exit because of his disappointment over not succeeding Dafoe (he would later join the *Montreal Star* as editor-in-chief), told Gray he should not quit because of Dexter. "Take the Ottawa job," he said. "That will get you out of Winnipeg, it will get you a lot more money, and give you a chance to establish down there. When you've done that, you can jump in any direction you want." Kay and the children were upset when Gray told them they were moving to Ottawa. But it was either that, he said, or quit the *Free Press* and do something else for a living. With no other options available, they left Winnipeg in June 1946, and Gray began what he would call "probably the shortest career in the press gallery of any correspondent within living memory."

The cause of Gray's involuntary departure from the *Free Press* in March 1947 was unusual. Instead of being fired for drunkenness or incompetence—the usual reasons for reporter dismissals in those days—he was fired for refusing to write articles supporting Dexter's views on how best to market the Prairie wheat crop. It was an issue that had concerned Gray since January 1945, when the federal Liberal agriculture minister, Jimmy Gardiner, introduced a bill establishing a minimum price system for all Prairie agricultural production in the post-war era. Gray supported the proposed minimum price system because he knew that western Canadian farmers had suffered financial hardship during the war when access to world markets was restricted. Dexter believed, however, that price guarantees only served to subsidize inefficiency. What farmers had to do, said Dexter, was figure out ways to make a profit out of lower-priced wheat. The fact that he and Dexter disagreed over this issue would have been of little consequence when Gray was on the *Free Press* editorial board and Dexter was the paper's Ottawa correspondent because Gray never had to write editorials criticizing federal policies that he personally supported. However, as the paper's new Ottawa correspondent, Gray was now expected to file stories bolstering the editorial positions taken by Dexter as editor-in-chief.

Things came to a head between the pair in early 1947, when

Canada signed an agreement undertaking to supply wheat to the United Kingdom for five years at prices well below those charged by other grain-producing countries. To Dexter, the wheat agreement was a betrayal of every laissez-faire policy the Liberal party stood for and a repudiation of the freewheeling multinational trade system he strongly supported. To Gray, who believed that laissez-faire policies only served to destroy the economy of western Canada, the wheat agreement was a logical extension of the minimum-price system that the federal government had already adopted. He wrote three articles putting forward this view and then moved on to other subjects.

The articles never appeared. Dexter refused to run them because they contradicted his belief that the wheat agreement should be scrapped. He spent the next few months writing editorials to this effect and then travelled to Ottawa to tell Gray what he expected of him as Parliamentary correspondent. The meeting did not go well. Dexter had spent more than twenty years in Ottawa supplying former editor, John W. Dafoe, with ammunition for his editorial positions and he expected Gray to do the same for him. In Dexter's view, there had to be complete agreement between the editor-in-chief and the Ottawa correspondent on all of the main policy points. He had no time for a rebel who did not subscribe wholeheartedly to his editorial line.

Dexter left the meeting thinking he had made his point and that Gray would see the error of his ways. Gray knew, however, that he could not write to order for an editor who believed farmers should make it on their own without government help. He knew the struggles of western farmers had started long before the Second World War, and he thought that a five-year period of minimum prices was little enough repayment for the years of suffering they had endured. The farmers had earned the right to say what kind of arrangement they wanted for marketing their production, and they had expressed strong support for the minimum-price system.

Gray never wrote another line in support of Dexter's free-enterprise views. The result was perhaps inevitable. In March 1947, Gray received a long letter from Dexter suggesting he look for employment elsewhere. Gray was a little surprised because he half expected Dexter to offer him a writing job back at the *Free Press* in Winnipeg. But he was just as relieved that he now had a chance to leave Ottawa because, during all of his time there, he had felt almost totally irrelevant as a correspondent working for a western regional newspaper.

Gray had discovered that one could almost spend an entire lifetime in Ottawa without knowing that western Canada existed. The only items of western origin that ever appeared in the eastern newspapers were sports scores and stories about natural disasters. The Ottawa newsstands did not stock western newspapers, but even if they had, chances are the politicians and bureaucrats would never have read them. This was a sobering discovery for Gray. In Winnipeg, Dafoe and Ferguson had given him to understand that the *Free Press* was a great national institution—a newspaper of influence and power with a long tradition of preventing federal politicians from adopting policies and passing laws harmful to the public interest. The reality, Gray discovered, was that the federal politicians only read the newspapers published in Ottawa, Toronto, and Montreal. None of them ever read the editorial page proofs the *Free Press* conscientiously airmailed to Ottawa every day. Even if they had read them, chances are the politicians would have paid them little heed. Editorial writers liked to believe their published opinions helped define government policy, but as Gray observed in *Troublemaker!*, they were only deluding themselves: "The constructive influence that all the editors of Canadian newspapers and magazines have had on national affairs since the sealing of Confederation would probably fit rather comfortably in the corner of a gnat's eye."

Nor did the politicians ever see the stories that Gray filed from Ottawa to the *Free Press*. He was operating in a vacuum, doing a job that he realized was about as significant as "writing on the ice in a spring thaw." However, he did make productive use of his otherwise wasted year in Ottawa when he wrote a draft of his first book, *The Winter Years*. The book, which would take twenty years to find a publisher, established the populist tone and vivid folkloric storytelling style for all the books Gray would eventually write about the history of the Canadian West.

Gray told his press gallery colleagues he would not be available for another parliamentary correspondent's job should one become available. ("I need not have concerned myself; none was ever offered.") Instead, in a move that foreshadowed what he would later try to achieve with his books, he decided to devote the rest of his journalistic career to "explaining" western Canada to the rest of the country. He would set himself up as a freelance "foreign" correspondent in Winnipeg ("a lot more foreign than being a correspondent in London, Paris or Washington") and write articles for *Maclean's* magazine, the *Ottawa Citizen*, and the *Montreal Star* that would make the transplanted westerners among their readers "feel a little more at home in their own country."

Gray returned to Winnipeg with his family in June 1947 and was about to launch his new career as a freelancer when he received a telephone call from a Calgary lawyer named Marshall Porter, whom he had met while covering a federal inquiry into the taxation of farmer-controlled grain marketing cooperatives. Porter had heard about Gray's dismissal from the *Free Press* and wanted to know if he would be interested in becoming the editor of the *Farm and Ranch Review*—a forty-two-year-old Alberta farm journal that Porter had just bought with two friends. As the solicitor for the Alberta Wheat Pool, Porter knew about Gray's sympathy for the struggles of western farmers and felt he would be a good choice for editor. Gray, however, was reluctant to abandon his newly acquired status as a "liberated wage slave." He was about to reject the job offer when Porter invited him to come out to Calgary— at the lawyer's expense—to meet with the partners and spend some time at the Calgary Stampede. "I accepted the invitation, and my life was never to be the same again."

A "Prairie Cassandra"
1947-1955

Marshall Porter gained control of the *Farm and Ranch Review* when the sons and daughters of the Calgary-based agricultural journal's original owner—Charles W. Peterson—feuded over the disposition of their father's corporate assets. Porter was the lawyer for the Peterson estate. When he learned that none of the children wanted to take over the family business, which also included Western Printing and Lithographing—one of the largest and most profitable printing firms in Alberta—he put together a deal to take the business off their hands. His partners were Gordon Love, the owner of Calgary radio station CFCN, and Robert Dinning, president of the Burns meat-packing company. Love and Dinning were interested primarily in the profits from the printing operation, while Porter was motivated by the opportunity to become publisher of the venerable farm monthly. A relentless optimist, Porter saw Alberta as being on the threshold of the greatest economic boom in its history, because of the big oil discovery at Leduc on 13 February 1947. He wanted the *Farm and Ranch Review* to become a significant forum for discussing such issues as the restoration of mineral rights to Alberta farmers and the conversion of resource development investments into tax shelters.

James H. Gray travelled to Calgary by train in July 1947 to accept Porter's invitation to be his guest during the Calgary

Stampede and discuss Porter's offer for him to become the editor of the *Farm and Ranch Review*. When Gray protested that his knowledge of farming and ranching was nonexistent and that therefore he would make for an incompetent editor, Porter told him that he wanted the *Farm and Ranch Review* to be more than just an advice journal with handy how-to tips for farmers and ranchers. "As a matter of fact, the less attention we pay to those so-called farm problems the better," Porter said. "What we have to do is raise the level of the farmer's interest in the great issues which are going to beset this country."

When Gray protested that he also knew nothing about oil exploration and mineral rights, Porter declared he was an expert in this field after having practised law in Alberta for more than twenty years. "I'll put a lot of stuff together for you, and we can get together for bull sessions," he said. "I know that in a matter of weeks our ideas will begin to meld." With the right direction, Porter added, the *Farm and Ranch Review* could become the "bible of western agriculture," as well read in western Canada as *Time* magazine and "a real power in the land."

At the end of the interview, Gray was ready to accept Porter's job offer, which would pay him a yearly salary of $4,200. This was $1,800 less than he had been receiving at the *Free Press*, but the offer also included a substantial block of shares in the company. "We don't want you to come out in the guise of a hired hand," explained Porter. "We want you to have a real interest in the *Farm and Ranch* and be one of the owners of it."

Gray knew that he faced trouble at home if he were to suggest moving to Calgary right away. Kay was just getting settled back in Winnipeg after their miserable year in Ottawa, and he knew that she would not take kindly to being uprooted again. The only solution—if he accepted Porter's job offer—was for Gray to commute to Calgary once a month to oversee publication of the current issue of the *Farm and Ranch Review* and to consult with Porter on the editorial content of the next issue. If that arrangement worked for a year, then Gray would plan on moving permanently to Calgary.

After the two men shook hands on the deal, Gray realized with some unease that he was accepting a job to edit a journal that he had never actually seen. In fact, he had never even heard of the magazine prior to Porter's phone call. That lapse was quickly rectified when Porter drove him over to the Western Printing plant on Second Avenue West to pick up some copies. Gray's first impression was not favourable: "An agricultural version of *Time* magazine it certainly was not." The journal was poorly designed and printed on cheap newsprint, and the editorial content consisted mainly of press releases from farm machinery manufacturers and government agriculture departments. A number of improvements would have to be made if this forty-page magazine was to become competitive with other Canadian and American farm journals.

Gray began by revamping the design of the magazine; dispensing with most of the handout material; and hiring freelance correspondents, such as future Alberta historian Grant MacEwan (then in Winnipeg, and, like Gray, a writer who had started his writing career during the Great Depression) and Red Deer conservationist Kerry Wood. Gray also recruited agricultural specialists to act as an informal editorial advisory board for the magazine. After consulting with Porter, Gray wrote all the opinion pieces for the magazine, and he spent between three and seven days in Calgary each month overseeing the page makeup for each issue.

After six months of commuting, Gray started making plans to relocate permanently to Calgary. He and Kay had discovered that the Winnipeg they had left in June 1946 was not the same city to which they returned in June 1947. Several of their closest friends had left town, and others were moving in new social circles. In the early spring of 1948, Jimmie and Kay drove to Calgary to look for a building lot. They found one in the upscale Mount Royal neighbourhood on a ridge overlooking the Elbow River in southwest

Calgary. They paid a building contractor $17,000 to put a three-bedroom house on it ("a hell of a lot of money for a guy like me to have invested in a roof and some walls," grumbled Jimmie) and listed their Winnipeg home with a realtor.

The Grays moved into their new Calgary house, at 609 Earl Grey Crescent, on 13 October 1948. A month later, Jimmie wrote to Sam Drache, his lawyer friend in Winnipeg, to say that the two younger children, Alan, age eight, and Linda, age six, had quickly adapted to life in Calgary. Daughter Pat, age twenty, did not like it at all. "She had too many friends in Winnipeg, and has not made any here." Gray had told Pat that her place was in Calgary with her family, while she said she wanted to stay at her girlfriend's home in Winnipeg and continue working at the job she liked—as a secretary at the Phoenix Assurance Company. "But she does have a job here now, as a secretary with the Canadian National Railway, and she is looking around for something more interesting."

Kay did not warm to Calgary either, particularly when she discovered she had to hike up the Seventh Street hill to her home after she had bought her household supplies at the shops on Seventeenth Avenue Southwest. "I drive up it in a car, but she has to walk it," wrote Gray in his letter to Drache. "It's a tough hill to walk, believe me. However, I suggest that the simple thing is for her to learn to drive the car. That will come with time, I guess." (As it turned out, Kay was never able to pass the test for her learner's permit.)

At the time of the Gray family's arrival, Calgary was starting to establish itself as the administrative headquarters of the Canadian oil industry following the big Leduc discovery of 1947. The population of the city was topping one hundred thousand; the first parking meters were being installed; and the Calgary Stampeder Football Club was about to bring home the Grey Cup for the first time. "Calgary is cavorting in the national spotlight," Gray would write in an article for *The Beaver* magazine after the 1948 Grey Cup win. "A whooping and hollering crew of Calgarians have taken a traditionally stuffy football game and single-handedly transformed it into Canada's outstanding national sports spectacle."

As the editor of the *Farm and Ranch Review*, Gray found himself in a situation similar to that of the editorial writers at the *Winnipeg Free Press* in the sense that none of the provincial and federal politicians to whom he dutifully mailed his editorials every month seemed to read or care about them. He also came to the sobering conclusion that the ninety thousand farmers who subscribed to the magazine did not much care about the editorials either, because none ever bothered to write letters to the editor about the viewpoints being expressed. Once again, he was operating in a vacuum, much as he had been as Ottawa correspondent for the *Free Press*. But that did not stop him from churning out a steady stream of clarion-call opinion pieces agitating for such benefits as a reduction in railway freight rates for goods shipped to and from Alberta, or the allocation of mineral rights to Alberta's agricultural landowners.

Gray later came to understand why *Farm and Ranch* subscribers refused to get excited about inequitable freight rates; the subject had been beaten to death by successive generations of politicians over the previous forty years. But he was mystified by their refusal to support his magazine's crusade to have mineral rights granted to them. Most of the landowners in Manitoba and eastern Saskatchewan held underground mineral rights as well as surface titles. Why would landowners in Alberta not want the same? A few lucky landowners had been able to acquire mineral rights from the provincial government for a small annual rental during the Turner Valley oil boom of the 1930s, and so were poised to collect big cash bonuses and royalties from the oil companies after the Leduc strike in 1947. But the majority of Alberta farmers got little more than token compensation for the nuisance value associated with heavy equipment being hauled across their land.

Gray noted that the state of Texas had dealt with the compensation issue by turning over seven-eighths of the mineral rights to the farmers who owned the land and appointing them as agents to negotiate whatever deals they could with the oil companies. He wrote several editorials urging that the Texas precedent be followed in Alberta. But the Alberta farmers as a group showed little willingness to fight for mineral rights, possibly because most of the drilling in Alberta was being done on provincial Crown land. When Gray's call for the allocation of mineral rights to the farmers fell upon deaf ears, he turned his attention to other natural-resource issues—including the question of how much natural gas Canada should be exporting to the United States.

The natural gas question came to the fore in 1950—after major gas reserves were discovered in Alberta and British Columbia—when the federal government passed three bills incorporating pipeline transmission companies. Two of the companies—Westcoast Transmission and Alberta Natural Gas—proposed to ship gas from Canada into Washington State, and this gave Gray an opportunity to become, as he put it, a "pro-Canadian voice crying in a pro-American wilderness." Natural gas should not be exported to the United States, he argued, until all Canadian needs had first been met. That meant that a plentiful supply of gas should be reserved for Canadian use, both as fuel and as raw material for petrochemical research.

Gray was not the only one calling for a restriction on gas exports. Elsewhere in Alberta, politicians and business people were publicly voicing their concerns about the petroleum industry. The Town of High River went on record as opposing gas exports until all the towns in Alberta were connected to a gas supply. The Edmonton Chamber of Commerce, the City of Calgary, and the companies that supplied the domestic gas needs of the province all joined the protest against exports. The Alberta Petroleum and Natural Gas Conservation Board soon got the message and ruled that gas exports would only be permitted when it was demonstrated that Alberta had enough proven reserves to meet its needs for thirty years. When the American petroleum regulators did something similar in 1951 by cutting off the flow of natural gas from the States into Ontario, Gray responded by arguing that no gas should ever leave Canada until the needs of Ontario and Quebec were fully satisfied.

While Gray's editorials about gas exports reflected what he perceived as the general mood in Alberta, his readers did not seem to share his concerns. The only time they ever became concerned enough to comment on the editorial content of the *Farm and Ranch Review* was when he printed a letter that he composed himself, using the pen name "James Henry" with a fictitious address in Lloydminster. This was a common technique used by newspapers in those days whenever they wanted to get some controversy going on the letters page. In his fake letter, "Henry" took issue with the journal's religion correspondent—Presbyterian Minister Frank Morley—for saying that the universal yearning for heaven was proof that humans possessed immortal souls. Gray, who had never been to church as a child and had embraced a humanistic form of agnosticism after some brief exposure to Sunday school, relished challenging the minister's precepts. His readers, however, were not amused. They sent in their angry responses at the rate of twenty to thirty letters a day. This finally opened Gray's eyes to the reality of where he was failing with the magazine. In his naive quest to turn the *Farm and Ranch Review* into the *Time* magazine of western Canada, he was blithely ignoring what mattered most to his rural readership. They might have cared somewhat about his deliberations on the great issues besetting the country, but clearly they cared much more about the teachings of the Bible. Gray's challenge was to find a way to make his editorials more meaningful to their lives.

The opportunity to draw more readers to the *Farm and Ranch Review* editorial pages came in 1952, when one of the principal investors, Gordon Love, began pushing for what in later years would be called "media convergence." As the owner of radio station CFCN, Love felt that Gray should be promoting the station's interests by using the magazine to attack the governors of the Canadian Broadcasting Corporation for restricting the ability of private broadcasters to make a profit. (The CBC governors were the national broadcast regulators in Canada then; they retained that responsibility until the independent Canadian Radio-Television Commission was established in 1968.) Gray did not think that radio-station profit-making was an appropriate issue for a farm journal, but he did agree to bring the two enterprises closer together by doing a twice-weekly talk show on CFCN entitled, "I'd Rather Be a Farmer."

The program name was not a gimmick. After five years of writing about agricultural matters, the boy from Whitemouth, Manitoba, really did want to get back to the land. He had spent many hours in the livestock barns at the Stampede grounds, learning from experts how to tell a good cow from a poor one. He knew how to identify the qualities that made for prize-winning bulls and superior horses. And he had done some experimental grass seeding on twenty acres of horse pasture that he owned on a rocky hillside on the western outskirts of Calgary, in what later became the Patterson Heights district of the city.

Gray had bought the horse pasture for two thousand dollars in 1949 to accommodate some saddle horses that he acquired, both to rekindle an interest dating back to his teenage years as a Winnipeg racetrack employee, and also to introduce his two younger children, Alan and Linda, to the pleasures of horse riding. He paid forty dollars for a horse at a Stampede spring sale, hired a man to train it, and then rode the horse himself for a few months to ensure it would be safe for nine-year-old Alan. The following year, he bought a pregnant mare at a Stampede sale of American Saddlebred palominos. The foal was to be for Linda, then turning eight. From the mare—named Halloka Gloria—Gray raised a palomino colt that won a reserve junior championship rosette at the Royal Winter Fair in Toronto in 1952 and was pictured on the cover of *Saturday Night* magazine. Linda named the colt Bambi, took lessons with Alan at a Calgary riding club, and later rode twice with her brother and other club students in the Calgary Stampede parade.

Gray bought the horse pasture—which overlooked the Bow River and had a panoramic view of the downtown skyline—from Rex Dwigans, a used-car dealer and oil patch speculator. Dwigans provided Gray with an unexpected fringe benefit when he gave him the opportunity to invest two thousand dollars for a 5 percent share in a wildcat oil well that proved successful.

Gray told friends that had he been able to afford it—though money does not really seem to have been a problem for him then —he would have given up journalism for farming in the early 1950s "because I was fascinated by everything about production from the soil." He also loved country living. In 1950, he and Kay sold the house they had built in Mount Royal, because they did not want to pay the high property taxes any longer, and moved into a smaller home in the Richmond neighbourhood of south-west Calgary while they built a new three-bedroom home on the hillside acreage where they kept the horses. Gray's daughter Pat, who married Calgary draftsman Bill Whittaker on 18 May 1951, recalls that when she returned from her honeymoon she found her father putting down the cinder-block foundation for the new bungalow, with Kay standing by his side clutching a book entitled *How to Build Your Dream House for $3,500 or Less*. The home took two years to build, with Jimmie and Kay acting as joint general contractors. Gray named the place Grasmere Farm after the tranquil spot in the English Lake District that was once the home of the poet William Wordsworth.

It now seems doubtful that Gray ever seriously intended Grasmere to be a farm in anything other than name only. His son, Alan, would later recall that the closest his father ever came to cultivating anything aside from oats for the horses was a failed attempt to grow mushrooms in the basement of their home. But Gray always talked about "the farm" as if it were a place where he eventually planned to have chickens and cows and crops, as well as pasture for the horses.

With no apparent desire to carry on any actual farming activity at Grasmere, apart from feeding and stabling the horses, Gray settled instead for talking about farming on his radio program, which he used primarily as a recycling medium for his editorials and articles from the *Farm and Ranch Review*. In one article, entitled "You could live a good life, in a friendly, peaceful world," he wrote admiringly about the homesteading era that existed before he was born, when a young person could become established as a farmer with little more than "willing hands, a strong back, and the determination to get a farm of your own." As Gray saw it, the early homesteaders were the spiritual antecedents of the self-sufficient individuals who succeeded in the bootstrap economy of the 1920s. They worked hard, found a way to make a successful living off the land, and came up with simple, practical solutions to their problems without any need for the "esoteric hallucinations of Socialism, Fascism or Social Credit." In the process, they earned the freedom to "do as they liked, where they liked and when they liked."

Gray did the radio show for two years until a broadcast about crow hunting set him at odds with the Alberta Fish and Game Association, a lobby group for anglers and hunters. In his commentary, Gray declared that crow hunting should be banned because it endangered a species that was an indispensable part of the bird kingdom. The Fish and Game Association—which regarded crows as unwanted pests—responded by threatening to boycott the products of the companies sponsoring Gray's radio program. The CFCN station management responded by taking Gray off the air.

By that time, in 1954, Gray was feeling more and more like a crusader without an audience, or as he would describe himself in *Troublemaker!*: "a Prairie Cassandra." After seven years of trying to improve the editorial quality of the *Farm and Ranch Review*, he was forced to admit that the magazine was still little more than a throwaway publication for rural subscribers. They kept receiving it for decades on end (one dollar bought a ten-year subscription) because they had once filled out a coupon in a circulation contest. Thousands of unwanted copies of the magazine were piling up monthly in trash bins in rural post offices. Requests to cancel subscriptions went ignored because advertising rates were based on subscription totals, and the goal of the *Farm and Ranch* advertising manager was to ensure that every issue contained at least 65 percent advertising. Realizing this, Gray often contemplated a return to daily journalism. However, because this would have meant moving to Vancouver or Toronto—where he felt the best newspaper opportunities existed—he never took that step.

Things came to a head in January 1955, when Porter became a justice of the Supreme Court of Alberta. Porter turned over most of his *Farm and Ranch Review* shares to his three daughters, while partner Dinning sold his shares to partner Love. At that point, Gray tried to cash in his own promised shares in *Farm and Ranch*, but Love refused to honour what had been a separate handshake agreement between Gray and Porter. Gray resigned from *Farm and Ranch* and asked his lawyer friend Sam Drache to help him extract a settlement from Love for Gray's promised shares. But the case went nowhere because Porter denied he had ever offered shares to Gray and there was no paperwork to prove otherwise.

Gray's departure from the magazine came just after he published a special issue marking the *Farm and Ranch Review*'s fiftieth year of publication. In his main editorial, he praised the magazine's founders for establishing the publication as an advocacy journal for western Canadian farmers, not as a publication to "teach farmers how to farm and ranchers how to ranch." He added that this philosophy (to which he wholeheartedly subscribed) undoubtedly contributed to the magazine's longevity: "At the very least, the oldest farm magazine west of Toronto should on its Golden Jubilee be permitted to claim special powers of endurance that many of its early competitors lacked." However, without giving any hint of his own plans to leave the magazine, Gray suggested that the road ahead might be "the rockiest trail we are ever likely to see" and that the seventy-fifth anniversary might be harder to reach.

After leaving *Farm and Ranch*, Gray accepted the job of editor at another Calgary-based industry publication, the *Western Oil Examiner*. His timing was fortuitous. Within two years, the *Farm and Ranch Review* was no more. Its "special powers of endurance" began to fail almost from the moment Gray left. It had lost so much advertising—mainly because of heavy competition from television—that it quickly lost viability as a profitable undertaking.

Adventures in the Oil Patch
1955-1963

When James H. Gray became the editor of the *Western Oil Examiner* in the spring of 1955, the thirty-year-old publication was changing from a weekly tip sheet for oil investors to a weekly petroleum industry trade journal that hoped to attract advertising from the various service and supply companies operating in the oil patch. Its publisher was Arthur (Scotty) Shoults, a Calgary advertising agency executive. Its chief investor was Robert (Bobby) Brown Jr., a shrewd oil patch operator who had pulled off a major coup in 1951 when he gained control of Home Oil—a Canadian company in which no single investor or group of investors held a majority stake—by the simple device of quietly buying its shares on the open market.

Gray told Shoults and Brown that because he knew nothing about the technical side of the oil business and had no news sources within the industry, he might not be the best choice for editor of the *Western Oil Examiner*. However, they assured him that such qualifications were unnecessary. In much the same way that Marshall Porter had persuaded him to take on the editorship of the *Farm and Ranch Review* seven years earlier, Shoults and Brown told Gray that they could provide him with all the expert help he needed. Gray's job, as they saw it, was to make the *Western Oil Examiner* the voice of the independent Canadian companies that were battling for survival in the American-dominated oil patch. With the market for domestic oil declining because of a surplus of cheap oil flooding into North America from Venezuela and the Middle East, Canadian companies were being forced to cut back on production. That was hurting their bottom line.

Gray welcomed the opportunity to pursue a pro-Canadian line in his editorials for the *Western Oil Examiner* because he had been doing the same thing at the *Farm and Ranch Review* for eight years. However, as he soon discovered, writing for a throwaway farm publication that often ended up in trash bins in rural post offices was quite a bit different from writing for a publication that circulated widely in the oil patch. He was now writing for readers who expected the weekly journal to focus on the positive aspects of the industry—not on any deficiencies it might have. They also expected the weekly's editorials to be couched in such innocuous language as to be completely inoffensive to anyone reading them.

On 5 June 1955, Gray published an editorial criticizing an American oil executive, Robert Wilson of Standard Oil, for saying that rigid controls should be imposed on all foreign oil coming into the United States. Gray argued that since some of this "foreign" oil was coming from Alberta, the province's economy stood to be adversely affected if such controls went into effect. A subsidiary of Standard Oil was already involved in the development of several oil fields in Alberta, so any move to restrict imports into the US would see the company cutting off its nose to spite its face: "It is a sad thing indeed to find such arrant expressions of economic parochialism in the very people we had assumed would be eager to protect their investment in Canadian natural resources."

The editorial caused an immediate uproar among executives of the big American multinationals operating in Alberta. They accused Gray of being anti-American and cancelled subscriptions. They refused to grant interviews to the *Western Oil Examiner*'s reporter, Rowland Hill, and they refused to give the time of day to the *Examiner* sales representatives who were hoping to bring more advertising into the magazine. With several competing trade journals, including *Oilweek, Western Miner and Oil Review,* and *Nickle's Daily Oil Bulletin,* already winning all the major advertising contracts, the fate of the *Western Oil Examiner* was sealed almost from the day Gray walked in the door. His attempt to appease the Americans by publishing favourable articles about their projects in Alberta (while simultaneously writing editorials criticizing American ownership of the resource industry) failed to bring in new advertising. The magazine's publication schedule changed from once a week to once every two weeks, then to once a month. Eventually—after three more years of struggling—the magazine ceased publication altogether.

The demise of the *Western Oil Examiner* came as no real surprise to Gray. The oil industry was already well served by the other trade journals, and there was obviously no place in an American-friendly market for a publication that adopted a pro-Canadian stance in its editorials. As Gray would write in *Troublemaker!,* he felt like a "silver-tongued orator at a deaf-mute convention." Things might have been different had there been some advertising support from Canadian oil companies to counteract the lack of support from the Americans. But the flow of advertising from Canadian companies that publisher Shoults hoped to develop through his agency never materialized.

The beginning of the end for the *Western Oil Examiner* occurred in early 1958 after Gray was recruited by the magazine's chief investor, Bobby Brown, to write a speech for delivery to a group of energy analysts in Toronto. Gray wrote about the need for a pipeline to carry Alberta crude oil to refineries in Montreal, where a potential market existed for two hundred thousand barrels a day. The speech brought Brown such a warm response from the analysts that afterwards he turned to Gray and said, "I know how to crack that Montreal market: We'll build the pipeline ourselves."

Gray had to admire Brown's gambling spirit. The Calgary entrepreneur had already committed Home Oil to investing millions of dollars in oil drilling programs at the Swan Hills and Virginia Hills fields in northwestern Alberta. He was also buying up millions of dollars' worth of shares in TransCanada PipeLines, a company established by the federal government to carry natural gas from Alberta to central Canada. And now he was proposing to build a $350-million pipeline that, as Gray would later write, "might have given the Shah of Iran cause for momentary hesitation." Not only that, but Brown was proposing it "with an air of enthusiastic euphoria found only infrequently in winners of million-dollar lotteries. He was the complete promoter."

If Gray had known more about Brown, he might have been more wary. The son of Robert (Streetcar) Brown, a hard-drinking wildcatter who made his fortune with a big oil strike in Turner Valley in 1936, Brown Jr. had a reputation for boldly going after big plays that made him a legend in the world of Canadian business. But his recklessness, compounded by his deepening alcoholism, made conservative Home Oil investors nervous. They felt that one of his gambles might one day blow the whole game.

The Montreal pipeline was shaping up to be such a gamble. But Gray did not know this at the time. All he knew was that Brown wanted him to immediately fold the *Western Oil Examiner* and come over to Home Oil as manager of public relations for the Montreal pipeline promotion. When Gray hesitated, Brown put all his cards on the table. His ultimate goal, he confided, was to obtain control of TransCanada PipeLines and move its head office to Calgary. Gray would then become the public relations director for all three companies—TransCanada, Home Oil, and the new Montreal pipeline venture—and he would be given a starting salary of one thousand dollars a month plus stock options. It was an offer Gray could not easily turn down, especially when Brown promised to soon raise his salary to fifteen hundred dollars a month—twice as much as Gray had ever earned before. He wrote his last editorial for the *Western Oil Examiner*—a Brown-pleasing commentary extolling the merits of the Montreal pipeline proposal—and began looking for a buyer for the magazine's printing equipment.

Before the Montreal pipeline could go ahead, it had to be approved by a Royal Commission established by the Diefenbaker government in 1957 "to investigate a number of questions relating to sources of energy." Brown and his fellow independent producers appeared before the commission to argue that the pipeline would open up an important new market for western crude oil and restore economic viability to the industry. Their opponents, the large American multinationals, argued that the Montreal refineries (which the Americans owned) would suffer severe hardship if the federal government forced them to substitute "expensive" Canadian crude for "cheap" foreign oil from Venezuela and the Middle East.

Perhaps the most influential intervener at the energy hearings, chaired by Brascan president Henry Borden, was New York petroleum consultant Walter Levy, who urged that the proposed Montreal pipeline not be built. Instead, he said, new markets for Alberta crude should be found outside of Canada while Montreal could continue to be supplied from existing foreign sources. The commission accepted this suggestion and recommended in its 1959 report that the American companies find new markets for western crude equivalent to what the Montreal refineries would provide, or else face restrictions on their Canadian operations. In addition, the commission recommended the adoption of a comprehensive national oil policy for Canada to be administered by a regulatory body called the National Energy Board. Gray would later suggest tongue-in-cheek in his book *Troublemaker!* that he should have received some of the credit for the introduction of the 1961 national oil policy (not to be confused with the much-detested National Energy Program introduced by the Trudeau government in 1980) because he had first proposed the idea in the pages of the *Western Oil Examiner*.

The collapse of the Montreal pipeline project left Gray with what he now viewed as an inconsequential public relations job at Home Oil. Brown's attempt to gain control of TransCanada PipeLines became an expensive blunder that cost Home Oil more than eight million dollars when TransCanada share prices dropped, so there was no opportunity awaiting Gray there. Nor, because of Brown's business losses, did the promised pay raise and stock options ever materialize. Facing a future in which he would have nothing to do but "attend meetings, drink coffee and read the newspapers," Gray began looking for a way to get back to what he called "the only thing a writer should ever do, because it is the only thing he can ever do: Write."

He found his opportunity at the end of 1963. On the advice of Calgary businessman John Scrymgeour, a former executive assistant to Bobby Brown, Gray invested in a Calgary strip mall. The income it produced, coupled with the returns from some strategic oil patch investments, allowed him to resign from Home Oil at age fifty-seven. He told a reporter for the Calgary *Albertan* newspaper that he planned to write a book about the impact of the Great Depression on the people of western Canada. He had written the first draft during the unhappy year he had spent working at the press gallery in Ottawa in 1946-47, and now it was time for him to revise it and try to find a publisher. The book would be called *The Winter Years*. He took the title from a poem by William Cowper, "The Winter Evening," which refers to winter as the "ruler of the inverted year." The parallel, in Gray's mind, was that during the Depression "all values were turned upside down."

The Winter Years
1962-1965

James H. Gray chose the Great Depression on the Prairies as the subject of his first book, *The Winter Years*, because he had an intimate knowledge of the subject both from having lived through it as a young husband and father struggling to support his family on unemployment relief, and from having covered part of the story as a reporter for the *Winnipeg Free Press*. The available written source material on the Depression was skimpy. The newspaper coverage was episodic and incomplete, and the reports of government inquiries into agricultural cooperatives, commodity price spreads, and federal-provincial relations were necessarily limited in scope. But Gray had his memories and his notes. He also had a considered plan of attack: His book would not be an academic study of the political, economic, and social forces that shaped the Depression; it would be a personal history of the Depression written from the standpoint of someone who had lived through it. It would be "undocumented by the voluminous footnotes that mark more scholarly works," he wrote in a letter to M. J. Coldwell, co-founder of the socialist Co-operative Commonwealth Federation party (CCF) that later became the New Democratic Party. "I am more concerned with the impact of the depression on people rather than in political movements as such. I will let the provincial historians do the documentaries, and I will concentrate on recapturing the flavour of life as it was lived on the Prairies during the 'dirty thirties.'"

Gray completed the first draft of his manuscript in early 1947, while he was still working full-time as a correspondent for the *Winnipeg Free Press* at the Parliamentary press gallery in Ottawa. A vice-president at Collins Press in Toronto told Gray that his company would be interested in publishing a book about Gray's relief experiences, and Gray spent the winter of 1946 researching and writing a sixty-thousand-word manuscript. However, two months after submitting the manuscript to Collins, Gray received it back with a printed rejection slip. When he phoned the Collins people to find out what was wrong, they told him the vice-president in question was no longer with the company, and that they had no interest in publishing the manuscript. Gray then submitted the manuscript to the Macmillan Company of Canada for consideration. Macmillan was the Toronto branch of an English publishing house co-owned by the future British prime minister, Harold Macmillan.

At that point, the book dealt mainly with Gray's own experience on relief in Winnipeg from 1930 to 1934, and did not cover the Depression story in the rest of Manitoba, Alberta, or Saskatchewan. Macmillan's Toronto president, John Morgan Gray—a history enthusiast with an expressed fondness for authors who could write history for a general audience—evaluated the manuscript and said he would publish it subject to certain revisions. Morgan Gray said that the author's newspaper training had taught him to write quickly, perhaps too quickly, and as a result his copy was superficial and filled with clichés—then the standard lingua franca of journalistic writing. In his editing notes, Morgan Gray described the chronological sequence of the storytelling as "a little confused," and noted that in a few places the author's anger, "which is still strong in him," caused him to lose perspective and impact. As an example, Morgan Gray cited a chapter about a female old-age pensioner who tried to find a husband through the columns of the newspaper with the stipulation that he, too, had to be receiving the old-age pension. "The author obviously enjoys telling the story," wrote Morgan Gray, "but he spoils it all by editorializing for about three pages on the pathos of the aged poor having to resort to such devices." (When eventually published, Gray's editorializing was cut to a single paragraph in which he wondered if this was to become the fate of all poor people as they aged.) Morgan Gray also quibbled with Gray's "free and colloquial" style of language, and suggested that such words as "yahoos" and "politicos" should be eliminated from the manuscript because they "cheapened" the writing.

Morgan Gray invited Gray to Toronto in the spring of 1947 because he was "most enthusiastic about the manuscript" and wanted to discuss "certain minor revisions." When Gray got there, however, he discovered there was substantial disagreement among Macmillan's commissioned readers as to what actual revisions were required. One reader, Gwyneth McGregor, even went so far as to suggest that Gray recast the manuscript as a work of fiction. "In that form, it would stand a chance of selling far better," she wrote. "For interesting as the book is in its present form, I cannot see a great many people buying it. Popular taste does not run to straight writing about events and problems, but coat the pill with the sugar of fiction and you have a great many more swallowers." Gray agreed to leave the manuscript with the readers while they made up their minds. Eighteen months later, he received a letter saying the readers could not reconcile their differences, and that Macmillan was no longer interested in publishing the manuscript. By that time Gray had relocated to Calgary, where he was editing the *Farm and Ranch Review*.

With Macmillan out of the picture, Gray struck a deal in 1949 with Winnipeg publisher Dave Simpkin to have the manuscript serialized by the newly revived *Winnipeg Citizen*, a newspaper that had first appeared in 1919 and then ceased publication for twenty-nine years. The plan was that *The Winter Years* would eventually be turned into a book, using the type set for the serialized chapters in the *Citizen*'s composing room. However, the plan evaporated when Simpkin ran into financial difficulties and stopped paying his suppliers. He found himself one night without enough lead to feed the newspaper's linotype machines, and had to melt down the type stored for *The Winter Years* book so that he could publish the following day's paper. Shortly after that, the newspaper folded for the second and final time. Gray then tried to strike a deal with *Maclean's* magazine editor Ralph Allen to have the chapters serialized, but this never came to anything–nor did his attempt to have CBC producer Harry Boyle turn the manuscript into a radio drama for national broadcast.

In October 1962, Gray decided to try Macmillan again. He still believed in the book and felt it would be easier to renew relations with a publisher who knew what the project was about than to start over with a new publisher. "I have re-read the manuscript in its entirety, and am still convinced that this is a chapter of Canadian history which ought to be somehow preserved," he wrote in a letter to Morgan Gray. "I believe the book should now be expanded and extended by an updating process. I am sure that during the next year the opportunity to gather the material required will become available to me. I don't write as well today as I did twenty years ago, but I still think I can do a workmanlike job on this project."

Morgan Gray was delighted to hear from his namesake. "I have wondered many times what became of *The Winter Years* and what became of you," he wrote in a letter of reply. "You will remember that we gave the book up with some reluctance, feeling that it had great merits. Certainly, we would like now to look at it again, and I would ask people who had not read it before to look at it now. We can see from that how it has stood the test of time, and what suggestions we might have for further work."

The initial response from Macmillan's commissioned readers was not encouraging. Three of them were against publication because they thought the Depression had happened too long ago. One, Des Sparham, dismissed the manuscript as the work of a hack: "An honest hack for whom one has a natural charity, but a total hack. He starts with a hackneyed theme and lacks the wit, the talent or the learning to play any kind of variation on it." Reader Ken McVey, a former diplomat and academic historian who would later become the editor of five of Gray's Macmillan titles—including such popular successes as *Red Lights on the Prairies* and *Booze*—wrote that it was not a book he could recommend to a friend: "Mr. Gray's memories of the depression belong more to a local history or an oral history project than to a general audience."

The Macmillan readers also had what Morgan Gray called "a serious doubt about the feasibility of revision." However, Morgan Gray told the aspiring author that Macmillan was still interested in seeing the rewritten manuscript after Gray completed his expanding and updating. Beyond that, the president would make no contractual or monetary commitment. Gray covered his expenses after he resigned from Home Oil by remaining on contract with the company as a freelance public relations consultant for a monthly fee of five hundred dollars, and by freelancing columns of political commentary and Prairie news coverage to half a dozen Canadian newspapers for a monthly retainer of one hundred dollars per newspaper. His daughter Pat, who was a secretary with the Calgary public school board, did his typing for him until the demands of her job, and being the mother of two children, became too much for her. "I would come home from work to find one or sometimes two articles waiting for me in my mailbox," she would later recall. "I enjoyed typing the articles as they were always most interesting and thought-provoking, but it was tiring. Finally, I said that I couldn't do this any more so Dad found someone else to work for him."

Gray spent more than two years adding to the original *Winter Years* manuscript by including statistical and other information drawn from government reports published in the three Prairie provinces, and also by incorporating statements from government officials on how they had dealt with the Depression, both publicly and privately. Russell Sheppard, who became executive secretary to Alberta Premier Ernest Manning during the 1940s, offered a personal reminiscence of the Depression that mirrored some of Gray's own experience:

> My most vivid memories of the depression centre on the great number of proud people who felt they humbled themselves by having to accept relief. It was the greatest blow that could come to many, and having to stand in line to have their shoes repaired hurt them deeply. There were many well along the road of life who were literally broken when their jobs disappeared. They lost confidence in themselves, and some never recovered to the extent that they could again take advantage of the economic upturn when it came. Quite a number I knew as a result of lack of confidence were unable to cope with their future, having always in mind the possibility of another depression.
>
> While the depression was hard on young people, also it was an experience that made them appreciate the better life when things improved. Those who had families to provide for, and had taken pride in their independence, were the ones who suffered greatly. I knew of one case where it was extremely humbling for the breadwinner to go from what was then considered to be a respectable job or position to shovelling out the gutters for relief.

While adding to the manuscript, Gray decided there were two abiding memories from his experiences as a reporter covering the Depression that he had to include in the book. Both came from the scorching summer of 1936, when he and fellow *Free Press* reporter Bob Scott drove across Saskatchewan in a *Free Press* automobile, staying at rundown hotels where they often found they were the only guests. The first episode had to do with a stop they made at a rural garage to have a swarm of dead grasshoppers removed from the radiator. When the proprietor finished the cleaning job, replaced the fan belt, and filled their car with gasoline for a total cost of about seven dollars, they gave him a ten dollar bill and told him to keep the change. He thanked them profusely for their generosity and then asked them sheepishly if they could break the ten dollars into smaller bills. "There was no place in the village where you could get change for a ten-dollar bill if you tried to spend it on anything," Gray explained.

The second incident occurred a little later in the day when Scott and Gray stopped at a farmhouse to get a drink of water. The woman of the house invited them to stay for lunch, and asked one of her two young sons to bring the men some water to wash up with. When they finished washing, Scott and Gray casually tossed the water onto the garden. The little boys ran to their mother to tell her in shouted whispers that the men had thrown the water away. She shushed the children by explaining that the men were from Winnipeg and did not know about saving water. The woman then explained to Scott and Gray that when one had to haul water ten miles, one learned to use it over and over. Water used for washing hands was always kept for washing clothes, she said. "Only after the water had gone through its complete cycle was it ever thrown on the garden."

After working on the manuscript for more than a year, Gray wrote to Macmillan on 30 March 1964, asking if the company was still interested in publishing the book. Executive editor Jim Bacque replied diplomatically, but still without making a firm commitment, that Macmillan was hopeful a "publishable" manuscript would result from Gray's revisions "and we are working with you as if we would publish it." Though the response was equivocal, this was sufficient encouragement for Gray to keep writing and revising. "The fact that you are interested in the project is enough to indicate to me that we have the basis for an understanding," Gray wrote, and he continued to work on the revisions.

By the time Gray finished updating and expanding his manuscript at the end of 1964, it had grown from 60,000 to 130,000 words—"the length of two novels," as a Macmillan commissioned reader would soon describe it. In a letter to George Ferguson, his former boss at the *Free Press*, Gray wrote that his examination of the back issues of the Prairie newspapers for the entire decade had led him to conclude that not one but three different Depressions had occurred during the 1930s. In Manitoba, the Depression had been mainly an urban problem. In Saskatchewan, droughts and crop failures had put one hundred thousand farmers and their dependents on drought relief for more than seven years. In Alberta, it was a Depression of surpluses: farmers had shipped plenty of produce to market only to discover that the money they received back was barely enough to cover their freight charges.

Gray's daughter Pat typed out the revised manuscript and Gray sent it off to Macmillan in early 1965. On 18 February he finally received the good news he had been waiting almost twenty years to hear. Morgan Gray wrote to him in a telegram: "If you are willing and prepared for massive revision of *The Winter Years*, with considerable help from us in cutting, tightening and rewriting, we can answer Yes!" Gray replied that he always planned to completely rework the manuscript anyhow, "so your use of the word 'massive' is only a little unnerving." When he asked if the person assigned to help him improve the manuscript would be an academic historian—because he feared seeing his narrative lose its garrulous flavour—he was assured by Jim Bacque this would not be the case. "The editor is a poet and magazine editor, not one of the university political science people," Bacque wrote, without naming the editor in question. "In fact, he is quite remote from academics."

A Prairie Historian Emerges
1966

James H. Gray spent most of 1965 working with different Macmillan editors to improve his writing style—which executive editor Jim Bacque described as "superficial, unoriginal and mannered"—and cut down the manuscript of *The Winter Years* from an unwieldy 130,000 words to a more manageable 90,000 words (about three hundred pages). This meant jettisoning some of the material he had gathered about the thousands of people who abandoned their Prairie farms because of droughts. He also deleted a number of oddball items, including a chapter in which he explored the claims—made by Alberta Social Credit Premier William Aberhart in his 1935 election speeches—that farmers had cooked and eaten gophers to stay alive during the Depression, and had burned barley for household fuel because they could not afford to buy coal.

Gray was reluctant to lose some of this offbeat material because, as he explained in a letter to Bacque, "in most of my writing I have been guided by the old vaudeville maxim: Never follow a banjo act with a banjo act." He wanted his book to be something more than an "endless chronicle of unrelieved disasters, which it might easily become." However, he agreed to cut the extraneous material when Bacque suggested Gray should forget about the mythical barley burners and gopher eaters and concentrate on exploring more important issues, such as the prevalence of anti-Semitism among Winnipeg employers during the 1930s, and why thousands of unemployed men trekked toward Ottawa to protest conditions in federal relief camps. (Gray would later incorporate the gopher-eating material into the manuscript for his book, *Men Against the Desert*, and even include some of the recipes that he collected for such delicacies as "gopher pie" and "gopher stew.")

After cutting several thousand words from the *Winter Years* manuscript, Gray began to have second thoughts about the editing process. In May 1965, he wrote to the Canada Council asking if it would be interested in sponsoring *The Winter Years* to the extent that "some of the germane material now being edited out could be re-edited in." He added that if the Canada Council approved his proposal, it would need to work out the details with his publisher. "But if you are interested, introductions can be arranged." When the Canada Council expressed no interest, Gray noted wryly that where federal grant applications were concerned he seemed to "fall somewhere between the imaginatively expensive scholastic boon-doggles and the unimaginatively inexpensive unscholastic boon-doggles."

Gray completed his final revisions in October 1965, turned the manuscript over to daughter Pat for retyping, and expressed to Bacque his concern that with the cutting and tightening of the text, "some flavour may have been squeezed out." However, a comparison of the final text with Gray's 1947 original version shows that his fears were unfounded. The core of the book was still the life-affirming story of how he had emerged from the ignominy of unemployment relief to create a better life for himself and his family; a story made stronger by the fact that it was now stripped of the anger and self-pity that had impaired the quality of the original. Additionally, it was the story of how he became a witness to history as a newspaper reporter chronicling the lives of people in urban and rural areas who faced the Depression head-on and dealt with it as best they knew how. Making his own experience a central focus of the book took a certain courage because it meant revealing aspects of a life of poverty and failure that others might have considered too bleak to talk about. But Gray thought it important to include his own story because it was the story of all the people who had hustled and gambled their way through the 1920s with no way of knowing what economic perils lay ahead. "What happened to me happened to everybody, more or less," he wrote. "There was nothing in our experience or in our history that prepared us for the Dirty Thirties."

The Macmillan people were pleased with the final draft. "The book as a whole is sound and full of interesting things," Bacque wrote to Gray on 25 November 1965. "I hope you're proud of it." Initial plans called for *The Winter Years* to be released in the spring of 1966, but the publisher decided instead to wait until the fall, when people would be thinking about Christmas buying. The official publication date was set for 30 September 1966—one month after Gray's sixtieth birthday. At an age when others might have been dreaming about collecting their pensions, the veteran journalist and retired public relations executive was embarking on a new career as an author.

Because he was still working as a journalist, freelancing columns and news stories to half a dozen newspapers across the country, Gray was able to attract a goodly amount of media attention for *The Winter Years*. Reviews appeared in newspapers from Vancouver to Montreal, and all were laudatory. Even academics writing in scholarly journals had good things to say about the book. Gray had been especially worried about the academic reviewers—because he was self-conscious about his own lack of scholarly qualifications and had intentionally aimed the book at a general readership—but the verdict from the academy was overwhelmingly favourable. The reaction of Michael S. Cross, assistant professor of history at Carleton University, was typical. Writing in the Fall 1967 edition of the *University of Toronto Quarterly*, Cross described *The Winter Years* as a "witty, touching and brilliant portrayal. No other book takes the reader so deeply inside the minds of the people who lived through the agony of the depression. No other source gives us so much appreciation of the heritage of that decisive decade. A minor masterpiece, it should be on the reading list of any Canadian who hopes to understand how this country has become what it is." Norman Ward, a political economist at the University of Saskatchewan, wrote a similar panegyric in the 15 October 1966 edition of *The Globe and Mail*, saying the book should be read by everyone who has ever had to ask, "What Depression?"

Two of Gray's former bosses at the *Free Press*, Bruce Hutchison at the *Vancouver Sun* and George Ferguson at the *Montreal Star*, also wrote flattering reviews of the book. Both described *The Winter Years* as almost unbearable reading for them because it brought back disturbing memories of how hundreds of thousands of Canadians were allowed to go hungry, ragged, cold, and hopeless at a time when the country had plenty of food and all other essentials of life. But they praised Gray for telling the story with verve and compassion, and for finding humour in the most unlikely situations. "The author looks back on his days of destitution with a wry merriment as if it were all a grand lark," Hutchison wrote. He recalled that when Gray was a young reporter, his "riven face, subdued manner and skeptical mind" all seemed to be products of his poverty-stricken past, and that his book now vividly recorded the horrors of that time.

Perhaps the warmest review of the book came from Scott Young, a columnist for *The Globe and Mail* who had been an eighteen-year-old editorial assistant at the *Free Press* when Gray was one of the rising stars of the newsroom. Young remembered Gray as "one of the characters, a jaunty slender man who could write like hell and was afraid of no one. He had been on relief in the early thirties in Winnipeg and if you have ever met a man who could joke about poverty and deprivation, that is the way he comes across in his book—which I think will endure." Young recalled seeing an early draft of *The Winter Years* when he was an assistant editor at *Maclean's* magazine in the late 1940s, and said he felt then that the wounds of the Depression were still so fresh that many who had been on relief (including Young's own family) wanted to forget or deny it "or at least not remind one another in a way that would set the scar tissue throbbing again." But now Gray had written a book that he "could stand on firmly if he never wrote another in his life. He writes with wit and a feeling for anecdote; but he also sees events against the big background of the nation. It is quite a combination."

One complaint about *The Winter Years*—made by a few reviewers—was that Gray had done what they considered to be a poor job of conveying the impact of the Depression on the rural population. "Gray has told the story as a city man," Barry Broadfoot wrote in the *Vancouver Sun* on 16 December 1966. "Some day, some farmer will sit down and tell his story." However, Broadfoot and the other reviewers did not know that the story of the rural population had actually been included in the forty thousand words Gray was forced to cut from the manuscript to bring it down to a manageable size. He would rectify this omission in his next book, *Men Against the Desert*, which would be all about the Prairie farmers who had battled dust-bowl conditions during the 1930s. In the meantime, *The Winter Years* was earning Gray national media attention and enjoying brisk sales. By Christmas 1966, with more than five thousand copies ordered and a second printing underway, it was already being hailed in publishing circles as a Canadian best-seller (defined then by sales of three thousand copies or more).

Men Against the Desert
1965-1969

Although he would tell newspaper reporters in 1978 that he had resigned from Home Oil in early 1964 just to write one book, James H. Gray was already thinking about a sequel to *The Winter Years* while revising that manuscript in 1965. Canada had been very good to him because it had given him the opportunity to rise from public school dropout to a position of journalistic responsibility and influence. Now he wanted to "put something back in the pot" by making another contribution to what he saw as the thinly documented social history of western Canada. He took the phrase about putting something back into the pot from the relief-camp strikers who had trekked to Ottawa in June 1935. Whenever they visited a hobo camp and found some mulligan stew in the pot, the strikers were always welcome to eat it. "But they were also expected to go out and scrounge something to put back in the pot."

Gray knew there were lots of histories written about great political forces, economic developments, and social revolutions, but very few about the men and women who broke the sod and laid the railway tracks. (Pierre Berton's classic books about the building of the transcontinental railway would not appear until the 1970s.) On 28 June 1965, Gray wrote to Macmillan president John Morgan Gray saying he believed there was a "great book" in the history of a federal government agency called the Prairie Farm Rehabilitation Administration (PFRA), established in 1935 to help farmers control soil erosion in the area known as the "Palliser Triangle"—a great swath of semi-arid farmland stretching eastward from Calgary to Morden, Manitoba, and southward from Saskatoon to the Canada-US border. This was a region that had faced virtual extinction as a farming area during the decade-long drought and economic depression of the 1930s. Settlers in the region had known almost nothing about agricultural methods that might be used for sustained crop production and had relied, for the most part, on farming practices that were suitable only for areas of higher rainfall.

Gray told Morgan Gray at Macmillan that the agricultural conquest of this drought-prone short-grass prairie area was a "wonderfully dramatic story of men against nature in the struggle to save western Canada from being transformed into a desert." However, he acknowledged that nobody would have known this from the PFRA files, which he described as "a record of monumental dullness, as all government reports are bound to be." To bring the story to life, Gray proposed chronicling the achievements of the agricultural scientists and engineers who had tackled the problems of soil erosion and dry farming in semi-arid regions and then worked with the farmers to develop agricultural practices and crops better suited to the prairie environment. Additionally, he wanted to tell the personal stories of the farm people who actually "went out on the land and did the job." The importance of the book was reflected in his belief that Canada could not have existed as a great wheat-producing nation without the settling and farming of the Palliser Triangle; and that Canada could not have survived, economically or politically, if this vast region had been allowed to go back to weed-covered wasteland and short-grass cattle range.

The people at Macmillan were reluctant to gamble so soon on another Depression book by Gray, especially since there was no knowing yet whether the early success of *The Winter Years* was a fluke or indicative of a public appetite for more books about life in Canada during the 1930s. "So far, we have not very much enthusiasm for the idea, or at least our interpretation of it," Macmillan executive editor Jim Bacque wrote in a letter to Gray in July 1965. "Our thought is that much of the best material is already in *The Winter Years*, and that a large part of the rest would necessarily be less dramatic." Gray's response was to pitch his book proposal to Western Producer Prairie Books, a Saskatoon-based cooperative publishing venture owned by a group of farmers who were members of the Saskatchewan Wheat Pool. Western Producer publisher Tom Melville-Ness accepted Gray's proposal without asking to see a manuscript first.

The core of his proposed book, which Gray would title *Men Against the Desert*, was the material he had gathered while updating and expanding the original manuscript of *The Winter Years*. As a result of that process, he had acquired enough material for two books. Plus, he had gained some knowledge of the subject both from having covered royal commissions on grain marketing and cooperatives as a reporter for the *Winnipeg Free Press*. He had also written extensively about agricultural matters as editor of the *Farm and Ranch Review*. The material Gray omitted from his first book, combined with the stories of the scientists and farmers who fought to save the land from dust, soil erosion, and grasshoppers, would provide him with plenty of content for a book expressing his conviction that the conquest of the Palliser Triangle desert was "the greatest Canadian success story since the completion of the Canadian Pacific Railway."

Like many Canadians, Gray had assumed before researching his story that the Prairie dust bowl of the Depression was a nasty quirk of nature that disappeared of its own accord when the droughts ended and the rains came back. However, he soon discovered that nature was just one player in the drama. Other players included the people who worked during the late 1930s at the agricultural research stations known as experimental farms. They were the scientists who developed drought-resistant crops, effective grasshopper control methods, and improved soil management practices to prevent topsoil from being blown away in black blizzards. Additionally, there were the armies of workers on relief during the Depression who planted millions of trees as windbreaks, built dams and rain dugouts to store irrigation water, and created vast community grazing pastures out of wind-blown wasteland.

Because he had spent $7,500 of his own freelance earnings on travelling and other expenses while researching *The Winter Years*, and did not want to be out of pocket again while researching *Men Against the Desert*, Gray applied to Canada's 1967 Centennial Commission for a $5,000 grant to cover his research expenses. He received word back from the commission on 4 April 1966 that it would approve a grant of just $2,500. "This will make the economics of the project pretty marginal," he grumbled in a letter on 9 April 1966 to Melville-Ness at Western Producer Prairie Books. "But it is something that I want to do nonetheless." Included in his research itinerary would be a trip to Montreal to "paw over the CPR library to see what literature they have on enticing the settlers into Saskatchewan," and a trip to Saskatchewan with a tape recorder to interview up to sixty people who had been involved with the PFRA during its early stages. (Gray offered to sell the tapes to CBC Radio after they were transcribed, but they proved to be unsuitable for broadcast because he had not held the microphone close enough to the people he was taping. The tapes ended up instead in the Saskatchewan Archives in Regina.)

Although he viewed the overall achievement of the desert conquest as a "wonderfully dramatic" story, Gray had some difficulty presenting it as exciting drama. The Palliser Triangle desert had developed slowly and spread slowly, and there was no climactic end to the crisis—only a gradual realization by farmers, scientists, relief agencies, and politicians that the desert had been pushed back. At one point, Gray thought he might find some drama in the story of ten thousand destitute families who had left the farms of southern Saskatchewan "and just moved north." But because the exodus had happened gradually over a period of ten years, and bore no resemblance to, say, the spectacular mass migration of farmers from Oklahoma to California described by John Steinbeck in his novel *The Grapes of Wrath*, there was nothing dramatic or exciting Gray could present here either. It was only when he zeroed in on some of the small, personal, heroic, desert-fighting stories that made up the larger whole—celebrating the achievements of the key individuals who performed nobly for little financial gain—that Gray was able to create the kind of drama he needed to tell his story effectively. His cast of local heroes included:

• L. B. (Leonard Baden) Thomson, the zealous administrator of the Swift Current, Saskatchewan, experimental farm who drove back and forth across southeastern Saskatchewan like an evangelical preacher, using films and demonstrations to show farmers how their land could be saved. In the process he became what Gray, with characteristic journalistic hyperbole, called "the greatest one-man faith-restorative that ever hit western Canada."

• Norman Criddle, the amateur entomologist from Aweme, Manitoba, who became such an internationally renowned expert on predicting grasshopper infestations that a Russian government delegation came to Manitoba seeking his advice on how to fix their grasshopper problems.

• Lawrence Kirk, the industrious crop breeder from the University of Saskatchewan in Saskatoon who spent ten years developing, from a packet of seeds he found abandoned in a desk drawer, a type of grass that would make better hay and pasture than the famous prairie wool that once covered the Palliser Triangle.

Gray worked on his research and writing for about eighteen months, documenting the battle against the desert with statistics, technical data, and anecdotes. When the book was published in November 1967, after a three-month delay due to production problems, he was most disappointed with the finished product. When compared to his first book, *Men Against the Desert* looked like a "badly botched textbook of forty years ago": a photograph of L. B. Thomson had been put on the dust jacket instead of Gray's picture; the typeface was poorly aligned; the text was riddled with typographical errors; the photo reproduction quality was poor; the wrong table of contents was inserted; and a map of the Palliser Triangle was omitted. Disgusted, Gray wrote to Melville-Ness suggesting that Western Producer, which also published a weekly farm newspaper of the same name, should get out of the business of publishing books if it could not do a more professional job of printing. Melville-Ness replied that while indeed Western Producer had made some mistakes with the publication of *Men Against the Desert*, it was not "quite as thorough a botch as you described. Our need was for better quality control, and I believe we have this largely corrected now." He rejected Gray's suggestion that Western Producer give up publishing books: "Our small publishing venture exists because we have a printing plant of our own and are fairly equipped with machinery to facilitate the manufacture of books. We will simply attempt to correct the things that appear to have crept up on us."

While Gray was still stewing over Western Producer's bungled production job on *Men Against the Desert*, he received a letter from Macmillan in December 1967 saying that sales of *The Winter Years* were approaching ten thousand copies ("exceptionally good for a Canadian book") and that "there should still be some interested Canadians who have not yet bought their copy." President John Morgan Gray wrote that the success of *The Winter Years*, following its initial rejection "and the long period of its premature burial, remains one of the pleasantest publishing stories I have had anything to do with—or indeed know." He told Gray he would be amenable to another book proposal should Gray have one in mind. Gray responded by saying that his next book would likely be a personal account of his early years in Winnipeg, set against a background of poverty, Prohibition, war, and labour unrest.

Gray was happy to hear back from Macmillan because he did not want to do another book with Western Producer. He thought Western Producer's distribution reach was limited, and he was disappointed that no marketing or promotion for *Men Against the Desert* had been done outside of western Canada. Even within western Canada, the marketing and promotion had been hit and miss because the company did not have its own advertising staff and had to rely on booksellers to publicize its titles. Gray's complaint about this provoked an angry response from Melville-Ness, who said that Western Producer simply did not have the resources to put on the kind of cross-country promotion that the larger Macmillan company could afford, and that the book-signing parties Western Producer arranged for *Men Against the Desert* in Regina and Calgary were going to eat up any profits that the company might anticipate on the first three thousand sales. "This is not a complaint," wrote Melville-Ness, "but simply to remind you that we, too, have one helluva big stake in *Men Against the Desert*. It's liable to pay off for you a long time before it does for us."

As it turned out, the payoff for Gray was slow in coming. *Men Against the Desert* sold just 668 copies in its first six months after release, for a net royalty return to the author of $330.66. (*The Winter Years*, by comparison, had earned Gray more than four thousand dollars after its first six months of sales.) However, sales of *Men Against the Desert* began to pick up as Gray heightened his media profile. In April 1968, he made a guest appearance on CBC television's popular panel show, *Front Page Challenge*. Two months later, he participated in a thirty-minute television documentary on the Great Depression that was made by the Ontario Department of Education and shown on CBC affiliate stations across the country.

He cut a dashing figure on television: *Calgary Herald* columnist Ken Liddell wrote that Gray's trim figure, steel-grey hair, and neatly trimmed grey moustache "could make a fortune for a man who wished to model for advertisements for fine whisky, good cigars, or well-cut suits."

The newspaper and magazine reviews of *Men Against the Desert* provided some consolation for Gray amidst his disappointment over the book's poor production quality and slow sales. Peter McLintock, writing in the *Winnipeg Free Press*, complimented Gray for effectively telling the story of "a great and, until now, vastly overlooked and underrated Canadian achievement." Tom Primrose of the Calgary *Albertan* newspaper described the book as "pleasant reading and educational." Grant C. Mitchell, writing in *Saskatchewan History* magazine, hailed the book as a "fine memorial to the key men in the struggle" whose legacy was the "prosperous farming communities in the dust bowl now producing food for a hungry world." However, some reviewers deplored the absence of a map showing the parameters of the Palliser Triangle, and said this could limit the appeal of the book for readers not familiar with the region.

The private reviews were similarly full of praise. Grant Denike, former employee at the Swift Current experimental farm, wrote a letter to Gray saying he had done "a marvellous job of putting together the various facts, points of view, motivations and strong loyalties during the formative and effective operational years of desert control." He complimented Gray in particular for acknowledging the leadership roles of such people as L. B. Thomson, and E. S. Archibald, the director of the federal experimental farms program who encouraged young scientists to think of themselves as crusaders working to raise the standard of living and add to the amenities of life on the farms.

In an effort to boost sales of *Men Against the Desert*, Gray's lawyer friend, Sam Drache of Winnipeg, wrote to former Prime Minister John Diefenbaker, urging him to read the book and perhaps provide a blurb that could be printed on the cover of future editions. Diefenbaker refused to give the book his seal of approval, however. He wrote back to Drache, saying he did not think it "properly reflects or gives a fair accounting" of his administration's efforts to solve the drought problem by authorizing construction of the Gardiner Dam on the South Saskatchewan River. Drache, in a letter of response, conceded that "in that sense, the book has some unbalance because it deals with a limited period and ends far short of Mr. Diefenbaker's administration." However, Drache added that the book should still be "in every curriculum in every school and every college on the plains of Western Canada."

Sales of *Men Against the Desert* eventually picked up—leading to a second printing of three thousand copies in 1970 after the first three thousand sold out. The book also earned the Historical Society of Alberta's 1967 award for "outstanding contribution to Alberta history." But Gray still considered it a relative failure compared to *The Winter Years*. "It's mainly about rural Saskatchewan and Alberta, and I guess farmers as a rule don't buy books," he said ruefully to *Calgary Herald* books columnist Reg Vickers. Nor did farmers necessarily view bureaucrats as heroes, though some of the bureaucrats mentioned in the book undoubtedly were heroes. Gray would later change his mind about *Men Against the Desert* and designate it his best book. But that would only happen after he had written four more books and had a chance to reflect on their relative merits.

The Boy from Winnipeg
1969

Western Producer Prairie Books took to heart James H. Gray's complaints about the production and marketing problems related to the publication of *Men Against the Desert*. In September 1969, twenty-one months after *Men Against the Desert* was published, A. D. Vick, manager of the books division at Western Producer, wrote to Gray to say that the company had completely overhauled the division to become a "fully-integrated publishing house." In-house marketing staff had been put in place so the company would not have to rely on booksellers to promote its titles. Sales representatives had been recruited to sell Western Producer books in eastern Canada, and the company's production problems had been fixed. Vick assured Gray that all typographical errors would be corrected and photo reproduction quality improved when *Men Against the Desert* went into its second printing in 1970. The Palliser Triangle map omitted from the first edition would then also be included.

Despite the improvements, Gray was not keen to do another book with Western Producer right away. (He would have three more books published by the company during the 1980s.) In fact, he was already taking steps to return to Macmillan, the home of his first book, *The Winter Years*. He had received a letter from Macmillan president John Morgan Gray expressing interest in doing another book with him. Aside from writing the book he had pitched to Morgan Gray about his Winnipeg boyhood, Gray was also toying with the idea of writing a work of fiction—a novel "about the struggle between good and evil among the tycoons of western Canada." (He would later tell fellow author Earle Gray that while he could think of plenty of tycoons who would be good models for villains, he could not think of anyone who could be portrayed as a hero.)

Macmillan executive editor Jim Bacque was not at all interested in seeing a novel from Gray. In a memo to Morgan Gray, he wrote: "I worry about someone starting to write a novel after the age of, oh say, eighteen. Jim told me he had a very hard time with *The Winter Years* because the writing proved unexpectedly difficult. He had not written for years before that. I have a feeling that we would only encourage him in agony if we got him to work on a novel."

With his fiction proposal thus scotched, Gray decided that for his next project he would, as originally planned, write a nonfiction book about the Winnipeg of his boyhood, covering the years leading up to the period he had written about in *The Winter Years*. Gray had no difficulty convincing Macmillan to publish what he would title *The Boy from Winnipeg* because he was now back on familiar ground as a writer of history and memoir and no longer proposing to move in an untried new direction as a writer of fiction. This time, there was no request to see a finished manuscript first. After scanning Gray's one-page book proposal, Morgan Gray sent him a telegram in July 1969 saying he was delighted with the outline: "Do start, knowing we are enthusiastic." He followed it up with a letter saying how sad he was that Macmillan had "missed out" on publishing *Men Against the Desert* and how pleased he was to be working with Gray again. (Morgan Gray was clearly unaware that Bacque, who had left the company in 1968 after seven years of "feeling like the parakeet on the admiral's shoulder," had rejected the *Men Against the Desert* proposal because he thought the subject had been covered adequately in *The Winter Years*.)

Gray told Morgan Gray that while his proposed boyhood

memoir would be primarily a first-person account of growing up in a "bawdy frontier boom-town" at a time when the local police ignored the proliferation of brothels, gambling dens, and bootleg joints, he wanted it to be "something a little more than a nostalgic excursion." On the one hand, the book would chronicle the adventures of the "Tom Sawyers and Huck Finns of Edwardian Winnipeg" like himself, but at the same time it would be a book about survival. Gray's life had not been "one long barefoot romp through Elysian Fields." It had been a struggle to survive in destitute conditions resulting from the fact that his father was a frequently unemployed alcoholic "whose trade disappeared with the arm he lost under a train." Yet, "kids have a survival potential that is beyond belief, and it's my belief that they survive poverty better than affluence," Gray told Morgan Gray. "If *The Boy from Winnipeg* is to have a theme as distinct from a message, I suppose it is that material possessions are irrelevant to the enjoyment of life during the discovery years of boyhood."

Gray took just three months to complete the first draft of the manuscript. He used the same storytelling style that had worked effectively for him in *The Winter Years*, combining detailed personal anecdotes with research data compiled from newspaper stories, census reports, Winnipeg city directories, and other written sources. If at times the personal stories—with their recreated conversations from close to sixty years before—seemed to border on the fictional, that hardly mattered to his Macmillan editors. The stories had the ring of folksy truth about them and that's what counted.

Gray was at his storytelling best when providing a boy's-eye view of events that shaped or touched western Canadian history. The chapter on what happened in Winnipeg during the First World War became the story of how his patriotic mother planted a "victory" vegetable garden on an empty lot and knitted thick socks and scarves to send to the soldiers at the front. It was also the story of how his pacifist father sided with the Germans because he hated the British for taking all the plum clerical jobs available in

Winnipeg. And it was the story of how nine-year-old Jimmie pretended to be a soldier by marching around the schoolyard with a broomstick handle for a gun. The chapter on the Winnipeg General Strike became the story of his unionized father sympathizing with the strikers and his practical-minded mother condemning the unions for insisting on job reclassifications when the employers were offering more money. It was also the story of young Jimmie enduring shouted abuse for delivering a newspaper that the strikers regarded as an enemy-produced publication.

In one chapter, Gray offered a revealing look at what it was like to be in a classroom of immigrant children ("a towerless Babel") at Machray elementary school, where the kids who spoke English had an immediate advantage over the youngsters who spoke only Russian or Polish. In another chapter, he touched on the roots of his agnosticism. He had never attended church as a child because his mother was a lapsed Presbyterian or Methodist (she could never remember which) and his father "didn't put much stock in any religion." (On their marriage certificate in 1905, Harry identified himself as a Methodist and Maria listed herself as Presbyterian.) But Gray did start attending an Anglican Sunday school in Fort Rouge, Manitoba, at age twelve, mainly because the church had a hockey program and a gym for playing baseball and basketball. The Bible classes focused largely on the miracles of Jesus Christ, and Gray's skepticism eventually got the better of him. Things came to a head one Sunday morning during an irreverent class discussion about the miracle of Gadara—related in the Gospel of Saint Mark—where Jesus exorcized evil spirits from a man and transferred them to a herd of swine that immediately ran down a steep embankment and drowned in the sea. Gray asked the teacher if the pig herder had been compensated for his loss. If not, said Gray, then his livelihood had been taken away from him and that surely was contrary to God's laws. There was also the issue of cruelty to animals that had been in no way responsible for the demon possession. After raising these questions with the teacher and receiving no satisfactory answers, Gray decided that skepticism was the only appropriate response. "The miracle business eventually nudged me into becoming a Sunday school dropout."

John Morgan Gray was pleased with the first draft of *The Boy from Winnipeg*. "In some ways it is very much about Winnipeg; in others it is a book about the wonder of boyhood," he wrote in a letter to Gray on 7 October 1969. "I think you have a delightful book in the making, and we much look forward to publishing it." The new executive editor, Manitoba-born Ken McVey, suggested that Gray could improve the manuscript by writing an opening chapter setting the scene for readers who might not be familiar with Winnipeg, and by incorporating more of his personal family history into the book. McVey also suggested that Gray should end the book at the point when he quit school and went to work. "That has both dramatic and poignant characteristics, and not only would enhance the chapter but is a story that should be told," McVey wrote in a letter to Gray on 19 November 1969. "This was a decision that no doubt a great many families in that time and in those circumstances had to make."

Gray spent four months working on the revisions to *The Boy from Winnipeg*. During that time, he wrote a letter to Morgan Gray saying that for his next project he wanted to write "the definitive history" of the oil and gas industry in Alberta. However, he lost interest in that project when the Government of Alberta turned down his application for twenty-five thousand dollars to cover travel expenses and the estimated ten thousand dollars in freelance income he would have to forgo while researching and writing the history. As an alternative, Gray then proposed to Macmillan that his next book be about prostitution on the Prairies during the frontier era, and be given the title *Sex and the Single Settler*. Morgan Gray expressed strong interest in this proposal, saying it could make for "interesting, valuable and entertaining reading." But he suggested that Gray pick a title other than a variation of the one used by author Helen Gurley Brown for her bestselling *Sex and the*

Single Girl. "What about calling the book, 'The Summer Years'?" he quipped. Gray replied that he would think of another title while completing work on *The Boy from Winnipeg*.

McVey wrote to Gray in December 1969 predicting that *The Boy from Winnipeg* would be a "great success." "There are books you like more each time you read them, and *The Boy from Winnipeg* is certainly in that category." The book was released in October 1970, just as Manitoba was starting to commemorate its centennial as a province. The reviews were as laudatory as those for *The Winter Years*. (Because *Men Against the Desert* had received limited distribution outside of western Canada, many of the eastern reviewers were under the impression that *The Boy from Winnipeg* was Gray's second book.)

The contributors to scholarly journals did not pay much attention to *The Boy from Winnipeg*, likely because on the surface it seemed to be more autobiography than history. But the reviewers in the popular press predicted that the book would become a valuable resource for future historians and for anybody who wanted to understand how the essential character of Winnipeg had been shaped. "The true and inner history of our country is recorded, not in Parliamentary debates and learned tomes, but in books such as *The Boy from Winnipeg*," reviewer Don McGillivray wrote in the *Edmonton Journal*. "His account of the searing quarrels in his home is better than a shelf of academic studies in revealing the impact of a general strike which was one of the turning points in Canada's history."

While Gray was flattered by the newspaper reviews for a book that in some respects he regarded as little more than a memoir to pass on to his children, he was particularly pleased when the approval of the academy came in the form of the University of British Columbia's 1970 medal for popular biography. "*The Boy from Winnipeg* rings with historical authenticity," said the accompanying citation. "Few writers commenting on the twenties, thirties and forties can match Gray's wit, his perception of what was actually going on around him, and his presentation of attitudes and facts."

Red Lights on the Prairies
1971

The idea for James H. Gray's book about the history of prostitution on the Prairies came to him when he was in Winnipeg in 1969, checking on some basic factual material that he planned to include in *The Boy from Winnipeg*. While looking through the back issues of the *Winnipeg Free Press* to verify dates of historic events, he came across a reference to a city police commission decision in 1909 to set aside a section of north Winnipeg—within walking distance of the Canadian Pacific Railway station and the Main Street hotels—as a segregated district where brothel owners could operate without fear of prosecution. Gray knew about this district from having been taken there at age thirteen for a sexual initiation that never occurred, but he did not know then that an official policy of toleration for whorehouses existed.

When he mentioned his discovery to some friends at the Winnipeg Press Club, they told him that Moose Jaw, Edmonton, and Calgary also had officially sanctioned red-light districts during the First World War era. In Calgary, for example, some of the brothels were situated on Nose Creek Hill, where the neighbours thought they were living next to "a girls' college of some kind" and where the future managers of the *Calgary Herald* would stake out the location for an imposing new red-brick newspaper building during the late 1970s. Because the subject had never been covered before, Gray decided to write a book about prostitution in the early West. No history of western Canada had ever dealt with the sexual activities of the pioneers. Gray noted sardonically that the existing histories would have you believe the West had been settled by "monks, eunuchs and vestal virgins." So here was another opportunity for him to make what he thought would be a useful contribution to the catalogue. He would take great delight in dispelling all the myths about upstanding Bible-reading settlers and telling the story of the raunchiest period in the history of the prairie provinces—when the proliferation of brothels "stirred the guardians of public morality to outraged protest."

Gray started working on the book—which he retitled *Red Lights on the Prairies* after John Morgan Gray said he would not accept *Sex and the Single Settler*—just as a new wave of Canadian nationalism was hitting its peak. Canada's one-hundredth birthday and the success of Expo '67 had given the nation a good feeling about itself. Everyone had learned the words to the Bobby Gimby centennial song, "Ca-na-da" ("four little, five little, six little provinces . . . ") and there was a great thirst for books about the country's past. It seemed the right time for Gray to begin writing a book about the sex lives of the men who filled up the empty land after the national railway was built.

To research the book, Gray spent more than three hundred hours poring over microfilmed copies of newspapers published in Winnipeg, Regina, Saskatoon, Moose Jaw, Calgary, Edmonton, Lethbridge, and Drumheller. "The old newspaper files are gold mines for anyone with strong eyes and a driven passion for Prairie history," he told *Calgary Herald* columnist Ken Liddell. "It's a matter of turning the handle until you find some obscure but pertinent paragraph. Couple one with another, and you are led from city to city in pursuit of the story."

From Liddell and from Pierre Berton, who had written about the building of the Canadian Pacific Railway (CPR) in his recently published book, *The National Dream*, Gray learned that "tents of prostitution" were established at construction camps all along the line while the railway was being built. From the files of the Methodist Church, he learned about the efforts of the Church's Board of Temperance and Moral Reform to curb prostitution in the different prairie towns and cities. From the municipal police departments in eight prairie cities and towns, he received statistics for arrests on morals and liquor-related charges between 1900 and 1925. (While the red-light districts generally flourished with the tacit approval of the authorities, including the Royal North West Mounted Police, itinerant prostitutes were often charged with the vaguely defined and loosely interpreted crime of "vagrancy." Madams were charged with bootlegging—an offence considered then to be more serious than prostitution.) From three dozen "ancient but lucid roués," who wrote to Gray after he made discreet enquiries in the letters pages of the newspapers seeking information on historic red-light districts, he received the kind of colourful detail that church reports and statistical documents never disclose—with the express understanding that he would never reveal the identities of his correspondents.

There was a certain amount of snickering from his press club buddies as Gray carried out his research. "How are you getting along with your fieldwork?" asked his Winnipeg pal Eric Wells. But Gray had no time for jokes as he conducted what he regarded a serious sociological study, tracing the links between frontier settlement, congested urban living conditions, liquor use, gambling, and the growth of prostitution. "Prostitution was the first major industry of the Prairies at a time when there were thousands more single men than women," Gray told a luncheon meeting of the Calgary Knights of the Round Table in August 1970. "The prostitutes were the real pioneers of western Canada." For virile young men seeking escape from cramped living quarters, a city's whorehouses were the next ports of call after the saloons and poolrooms.

Gray's personal interviews with retired police officers and former habitués of the tenderloin sections of the prairie urban centres served to give his manuscript a zesty flavour that the printed sources could not match. No civic report or newspaper account—with the possible exception of Bob Edwards's satirical *Eye Opener* in Calgary—could have told him that newsboys often made more money selling condoms than newspapers to railway construction workers. Nor could they have told him that a Moose Jaw madam named Rosie Dale established the first "U-Drive" system in her region by arranging for driverless horse-drawn hansom cabs to ferry her customers from the River Street livery stables to her home on the outskirts of town. The horses knew there was water and feed awaiting them once they got to Rosie's place, so all the livery owners had to do was point the horses in the right direction. When the customers were ready to leave, Rosie's houseboy untethered the horses and pointed them back in the direction of the River Street stables. Gray noted that Moose Jaw became the red-light capital of Saskatchewan at around the time in the 1880s when it was named the province's divisional headquarters for the CPR. An editorial writer for the Regina *Leader* newspaper later called it the "sin city of Saskatchewan" and "the Sodom and Gomorrah of the Prairies," while others dubbed it "Loose Jaw" and "Little Chicago." "Moose Jaw isn't a city or a municipality or even a geographic location!" thundered the anonymous editorial writer on 28 June 1921. "Moose Jaw is a goddamn virus that has permanently afflicted Regina and for which there is no known cure."

While the North West Mounted Police were responsible for enforcing the laws relating to boozing and prostitution, sometimes they became part of the problem. Gray discovered that entire detachments could sometimes be found passed out drunk in their barracks. "Single men in barracks rarely grew into plaster saints." One Alberta officer's diary was "a chronicle of non-stop poker games, fist fights, seductions, desertions and gang drunks lasting for days." When a certain Captain Jack was discovered drunk in bed with a Mrs. O'Neil at Fort Macleod, Alberta, her husband sued the captain for "taking his wife and keeping her" and was awarded $125 in damages. "An exorbitant sum," noted the diary of Sergeant S. J. Clarke. The miscreant officer, according to the sergeant, could have saved himself all that aggravation and expense if he had simply hired a Native prostitute at the going rate of three dollars a night. Even if he had been caught plying the prostitute with liquor, that would still have cost him only an additional three-dollar fine.

One of the more colourful characters Gray came across was a Calgary madam named Pearl Miller, who achieved semi-legendary status because of a story that started circulating about her after the Second World War. Gray could find no independent verification of the story, which told how a group of Calgary soldiers camped next to a regiment of American soldiers on the eve of the Normandy invasion in 1944. The Americans, who were fond of slogans, tacked up a sign on the wall of their sergeants' mess that read, "Remember Pearl Harbor." The Calgarians responded by putting up their own sign: "To hell with Pearl Harbor, remember Pearl Miller."

Gray talked to a number of Calgary veterans who swore that the Miller episode occurred, even to the point of saying that they actually saw the army signs. He decided not to believe them and wrote in his manuscript that the story was "obviously a fabrication." But he included the story anyhow because he thought it had the fundamental qualities of a legend and thus deserved to be repeated: "It could have happened. It should have happened. A great many people believe it did happen. In order to get a flat lie promoted to legend status, it must be repeated frequently. The story really ought to be true of a city where the most famous woman in its entire history was the keeper of a common bawdy-house."

Miller, who reigned as the queen of the Calgary brothels for close to twenty years, before finding religion and turning to social work, was the only madam who assumed any kind of human dimension in Gray's manuscript. The others existed only as names drawn from court dockets or from the selective memories of retired vice squad officers and former clients. One can easily understand why. Madams were not given to issuing press releases or granting interviews to the popular press. While he came across plenty of good anecdotal material to enliven his narrative, such as the story of "Big Nellie" Webb, an Edmonton madam who used a gun to protect herself from the drunken Mounties who were her most troublesome clients, Gray never managed to get a sense of who these women were, or how they ended up becoming brothel operators. Most of the madams in his book, like the prostitutes who worked for them, remained shadowy figures on the margins of the story. His sketchy description of Diamond Dolly, a Calgary madam who held sway as queen of the fleshpots before Pearl Miller arrived, was typical: "She was just Diamond Dolly, whose beginning—and end—are as clothed in mystery as her real name."

With the madams necessarily confined to cameo roles due to the absence of available biographical information, Gray gave the leading roles in his narrative to the larger-than-life police chiefs, magistrates, politicians, and social reformers who dominated the news across the Prairies when wide-open drinking, gambling, and prostitution were the order of the day. These included the likes of:

• Frederick B. DuVal, the zealous Presbyterian preacher who fought a successful campaign to close Winnipeg's Thomas Street brothels only to see the madams relocate their operations—with full police approval—to a new red-light district on Annabella Street and the adjoining McFarlane Street.

• Walter Johnson, the corrupt and untouchable Moose Jaw police chief who grew rich on graft and protection money for twenty years and eventually, at age seventy-seven, ran successfully for mayor.

• Nicholas Flood Davin, the hypocritical Regina newspaper publisher who refused to let stories about police brothel raids appear in the *Leader* because "the less families read of that unsavoury subject the better."

• Joe Clarke, the pugilistic Edmonton alderman and mayor, who thwarted various police chiefs in their efforts to curb prostitution and gambling because he wanted Edmonton to be like the wide-open Klondike of his youth.

• T. Mayne Daly, the tough-as-nails Winnipeg magistrate who sent robbers and burglars to jail for up to fifteen years but ruled that "all matters relating to houses of ill fame and immoral women be left to the chief of police, he to act in accordance with his discretion and best judgment."

To show where the brothels were located in the major cities of the Prairies, Gray supplied seven maps. He found one of them among the papers of James Shaver Woodsworth, a Methodist minister who went on to become the first leader of the federal Co-operative Commonwealth Federation (later the New Democratic Party). On this 1910 map, Woodsworth identified Winnipeg's fifty brothels euphemistically as "disorderly houses." At the time Woodsworth drew his map, the Thomas Street brothels in Winnipeg had been shut down and the street itself was attempting to regain a measure of respectability under a new name: Minto Street. "Somebody at city hall clearly had a most ribald sense of humour," observed Gray. "The Earl of Minto was Canada's most colourful Governor General." Appointed in 1898 at age fifty-three, Minto was known as a lacrosse and skating enthusiast who hosted many parties at Rideau Hall, described afterwards by guests as "lively."

Gray concluded from his research that prairie brothels operated more as adjuncts to a thriving liquor trade than as "independently functioning instruments of Satan." As a result, he gathered more information about the ban-the-bars crusades that preceded Prohibition than he could practically include in one two-hundred-page volume. In the same way that his research for *The Winter Years* had yielded enough material to form the core of his second book,

Men Against the Desert, his research for *Red Lights* provided him with enough data to get a head start on his next book, *Booze: The Impact of Whisky on the Prairie West*.

On 7 August 1970, Gray wrote to Macmillan executive editor Ken McVey to say that, for the first time with one of his books, he was going to include footnotes in *Red Lights* because "it will be a completely original work of historic research." McVey replied approvingly that this would allow Macmillan to promote the book as a "serious and challenging piece of social history." Privately, however, McVey was having major doubts as to whether, in fact, *Red Lights* would ever be a publishable manuscript because Gray had "failed to deliver the goods on prostitution on the Prairies." He suggested in a memo to Morgan Gray that they send it to Michael Bliss, a professor of history at the University of Toronto, for an outside opinion.

Bliss replied on 29 October 1970 in a letter that undoubtedly swung the publication decision in Gray's favour:

> There shouldn't be any thought given to rejecting this manuscript. Its subject alone guarantees profitable sales. But it has the added virtue of containing enough original material to fulfill the promise of its title. No reader will justly be able to claim that Mr. Gray hasn't delivered the goods. In fact, as an historian who has tried to wander about in this field, I suspect that Mr. Gray has delivered about all that can be found in the sources on his subject, and it would be unrealistic to think that there is much more to be said.

(Bliss would recall later that he had found little to write about when he first looked into the subject of early prostitution in Canada, and that he was most impressed by the quality of Gray's research: "It was astonishing to see how much information Jim had come up with.")

Encouraged by Bliss's positive response, Morgan Gray wrote to the author to say he believed that *Red Lights* would "polish into a characteristically entertaining and valuable Jim Gray book." The publication date was set for 1 October 1971, and the advance buzz in Canadian book circles was that this would be Gray's most popular book to date. (He had been shrewdly whetting the public appetite for the book for more than a year by talking to community groups and giving newspaper interviews about the "easy ladies" who helped settle the West.) Calgary bookseller Evelyn de Mille ordered five hundred copies and predicted *Red Lights* would outsell *The Winter Years*. To publicize the book, Gray embarked on a six-city promotional tour that, at age sixty-five, he found "arduous and tortuous." But it paid off in results. By 15 November 1971, *Red Lights* was riding high on top of the *Toronto Star's* national bestseller list—the only such list at that time—and sales of the book in Calgary were outpacing those of *The Last Spike*, the second volume of Pierre Berton's popular history of the CPR.

The newspaper reviews of *Red Lights* were generally favourable. Andrew Snaddon wrote in the *Edmonton Journal* that Gray had done his part to "make our lively history more factual," and reviewer Carol Caney suggested tongue-in-cheek in the *Albertan* that the City of Calgary should put a replica whorehouse in Heritage Park, the city's restored pioneer village. However, the academic reviewers were not impressed by Gray's attempt to produce what he called a "serious and challenging piece of social history." McGill University's John Herd Thompson, writing in the *Canadian Historical Review*, mildly complimented Gray for producing a "lively and amusing" survey of prostitution in the western provinces, but then criticized him for allegedly mocking the "deeply held convictions of the western reform movement" and for ignoring the impact of syphilis and gonorrhea on the settler population: "Surely two-hundred pages on pre-penicillin prostitution in which the words 'venereal disease' appear only once can hardly pretend to be credible social history." Gray pointed out in a politely worded response to the *Canadian Historical Review* that venereal disease had never been an issue during the period covered by his book because it did not become an item of concern to government health agencies until the 1920s. It was only then that the disease became reportable, and the first public treatment centres were opened.

On 22 November 1971, Macmillan vice-president Hugh Kane, a former McClelland & Stewart executive recruited as heir apparent to the retiring sixty-four-year-old president, John Morgan Gray, wrote a letter to Gray urging him to let American publishers of mass-market paperbacks bid for the rights to publish *Red Lights* in the States. Kane, an aggressive salesman in the tradition of his former boss, Jack McClelland, predicted that a paperback edition would sell at least twenty thousand, and probably as many as fifty thousand copies. Gray replied that he did not want to have his name associated with the "garbage end of the publishing trade," but relented when Kane told him that the New American Library was willing to bump up its print run to one hundred thousand copies.

Gray soon regretted his decision to let Macmillan sell the paperback rights to *Red Lights*. When the New American Library edition appeared in 1973, it was placed on the paperback racks next to *The Happy Hooker*, Xaviera Hollander's racy memoir of her life as a New York call girl. On the cover, *Red Lights* was billed as a book about the "bonanza years when the wide-open frontier was a hooker happy hunting ground." Gray complained bitterly to Kane about the New American Library's "burlesque" treatment of what he considered a serious study of prostitution on the Canadian Prairies, but Kane said that Macmillan had no control over the way the book was handled once the contract with the American paperback publisher was signed. Gray replied that this was an issue he would be bringing before the then recently established Writers' Union of Canada, a national organization of professional authors that he had helped found a few months previously: "I will be demanding a new deal for authors in the paperback world."

Booze
1972

As was the case when he did the final rewrites on his first book, *The Winter Years,* in 1965, James H. Gray was already contemplating one more book—possibly his last, he said—while revising the manuscript of *Red Lights on the Prairies* in 1971. "I promise myself that when I finish the whisky saga, I'll quit forever," he wrote in a letter to Peter C. Newman, editor of *Maclean's* magazine. "But that was what I said when I finished *The Boy from Winnipeg.* All authors lie to themselves, I guess."

Gray pitched his proposal for the whisky saga, which he called "my booze book," to retiring Macmillan president John Morgan Gray on 26 May 1971. It would be another book, he said, to shatter the myth that the West was a "somber, brooding place populated by grain elevators and taciturn farmers"; a lively book about the impact of whisky on the settlement of the Prairies—"the only frontier in the world which had Prohibition before it had people settling the land." Morgan Gray replied that any book suggestion from Gray was "always interesting and welcome" and if Gray decided to proceed, "I am sure it would end up a good book—valuable and popular." But he had certain questions and reservations:

Is there any particular reason for doing a book on booze in the Prairies, or booze in the West, or do you, in fact, propose

to do it for the whole country? Apart from any other consideration, I think it would be difficult to separate the operation of the temperance movement in the West from its
roots in the East and, I suppose, in the United States.

At the moment, I don't quite see the whole thrust of the
book, and how you would tackle it, but I am sure you have
ideas already, and that they would develop as your work
went on.

Morgan Gray, in what would prove to be a prescient comment,
also warned Gray that he would need to tread carefully in his han-
dling of the Bronfman family, who had risen from selling firewood
and fish around the villages of central Manitoba to turning the
House of Seagram company into one of the world's largest liquor
empires: "The law of libel would be leering over your shoulder in
that part of the story." But he added, "If you are interested, we are."

Gray acknowledged that the book might be problematic. But
not, he said, because of any potential libel threat from the
Bronfmans—whose activities as Prairie liquor peddlers during
American Prohibition were all a matter of public record anyhow.
He saw a greater difficulty in trying to seamlessly mesh the history
of the temperance movement with the story of how several governments dealt with what clearly was an enormous social problem.
He also wondered how he might obtain reliable first-hand
accounts of the booze-related experiences of western Canadians
who, as Gray would say in his introduction to the book, seemed up
to that point to have been "engaged in a massive conspiracy to
bury their past." But he planned to proceed with the research
regardless. He wrote letters to Prairie newspapers inviting readers
to share information with him—a strategy that had produced some
good results when he was researching *Men Against the Desert* and
Red Lights—and he wrote letters to Seagram asking for information about the early days of the Bronfman enterprises.

When he started his research, Gray was under the impression, like most Canadians, that Prohibition had been a great social disaster in western Canada. The conventional belief, fuelled by stories of American gangsterism in the 1920s, was that Prohibition had ushered in an era of gang wars, murders, and bootlegging on a large scale. It was also believed that Prohibition had been promoted by the Women's Christian Temperance Union, foisted on an unsuspecting Canadian public when the men were off fighting the First World War, and quickly repealed when the troops came home. The reality, as Gray discovered, was far different: "That this has become a basic of the Canadian credo is indicative only of our overwhelming passion for grafting Canadian conclusions onto American premises, and confusing Canadian reality with American mythology."

He discovered that in 1915 and 1916, the people of Manitoba, Saskatchewan, and Alberta had voted overwhelmingly in favour of Prohibition (205,000 votes for, and 88,000 votes against). While it did give rise to some bootlegging activity and armed confrontations between police and rum-runners in such isolated areas as the Crowsnest Pass near the Alberta-British Columbia border, Prohibition also brought a vast range of social benefits. The crime rate was halved, savings in banks doubled, jails were closed, and the Salvation Army's domestic-violence caseload dwindled. In 1920, long after the troops came home from the war, the Canadian electorate voted to further restrict the use of alcohol by stopping the flow of liquor across provincial borders. Three years later, in 1923, they finally did vote to end Prohibition, but only because by that time it had become a gigantic failure. Conflicting federal-provincial regulations; loopholes in the law that allowed doctors and druggists to dispense booze legally; and bootlegging, smuggling, and corrupt officials had all combined to make a sham out of the great social experiment. But that is not to say the voters wanted a return to the bad old days, when grocery stores sold booze for a dollar a bottle and saloons existed for the sole purpose of letting customers drink standing up until drunk. The voters wanted their provincial governments to regulate the liquor trade through tougher licensing laws, and to sell beer and spirits through government-operated liquor stores rather than grocery stores or drugstores.

Writing the book was a challenge for Gray because the history of drinking in the prairie provinces was much more complex than the history of prostitution. As William French would note in his review of the book in *The Globe and Mail* on 28 October 1972, "It takes a persistent man to unravel all the legislative entanglements, and the attempt is apt to become dull, to say nothing of disorganized." Plus, Gray had to deal with the problem of weaving the Bronfman story into the history, and to do so seamlessly and coherently without making it seem as if he was writing about two different subjects. "I have to keep going back to pick up threads," he wrote in a letter to Macmillan vice-president Hugh Kane on 25 January 1972. "When I finish the Bronfman chapters, which I carry through from their arrival [in Yorkton, Saskatchewan, in 1904] to their departure [for Regina in 1921], I have to go back into the middle of the Prohibition era and take up the story of the conspiracy of the liquor interests to bring back legal booze. I am sure it will handle well enough, but I worry about such things."

In the opinion of Macmillan executive editor Ken McVey, Gray's marriage of the two stories worked very well. "After reading through the revised manuscript," McVey wrote on 3 May 1972, "I am even more convinced that we have another winner on our hands." Privately, however, he was plagued with the same doubts he had initially harboured about some of Gray's previous manuscripts. "This book seems to have the same sort of virtues and defects as the original *Red Lights*," he wrote in an internal memo to Morgan Gray. "There's some great material, but it's a bit loose and repetitious. The repetition is not as serious as in *Red Lights* but there is a similar problem in the discussion of liquor legislation. I think it's unnecessarily detailed and confusing."

Finding a title for the book also proved to be problematic. For the longest time, McVey wanted to call it "Lips That Touch

Liquor," from the title of a sentimental 1900 poem by George W. Young, "The Lips That Touch Liquor Will Never Touch Mine," that Gray had mentioned in *The Boy from Winnipeg*. But Gray insisted that he wanted to have the word "booze" in the title. McVey eventually relented and agreed to what now seems like an obvious solution: Gray's "booze book" would be titled, simply, *Booze*.

Because he knew the Bronfman material could be potentially dangerous, especially because he planned to mention that one of the company's founding brothers, Harry Bronfman, had once been arrested and then acquitted on a charge of trying to bribe a customs officer, Gray sent the chapters to his Winnipeg lawyer friend Sam Drache for review. Drache replied with an assurance that he could not see any problems with the Bronfman material. "As long as what you have said is fully backed up, then you are merely recounting history in your own language," he wrote. "I must admit it makes very funny reading, though." The Bronfman people were not amused, however. They got an advance look at Gray's manuscript when a Macmillan salesman in Montreal gave the galley proofs to a chain bookseller, Louis Melzack of Classic Books, who then passed the proofs on to the Bronfmans for their comments. Melzack's reason for doing this, he said later, was that he did not want to have any book in his Montreal stores that might offend members of the Bronfman family—who happened to live in Montreal.

Gray received his first indication of possible trouble ahead in a letter from Hugh Kane on 11 August 1972. Macmillan had received the galley proofs back from lawyer Philip Vineberg—representing the Bronfman family—with certain passages marked to indicate what Vineberg considered would be objectionable to members of the family. These included a number of conversational quotes that Vineberg regarded as anti-Semitic. He also objected to a statement by Gray that one of the clan had a "withered" arm (Gray later agreed to change the word to "weakened"), and a passing reference to what Gray acknowledged was a "well-known myth" about an alleged murder trial and jury-tampering case dating back to the time when the Bronfmans were selling spirits through the mail. After passing along Vineberg's comments, Kane noted ominously that Classic Books had served notice that the chain would not buy or distribute a single copy of *Booze* if the Bronfmans were unhappy with it.

The timing of the Vineberg letter could not have been worse. *Booze* was due to be published in two months, on 20 October 1972; a first print run of 10,000 copies had been ordered; and advance purchase orders for 3,700 copies had been requested. Any move to restrict sale or distribution of the book would have been devastating. Or so Kane thought. Gray, however, saw this as an opportunity to publicly vent his anger about the threatened boycott and get some free promotion for his book. If the Montreal bookseller went ahead with his threat, Gray intended to employ his own strategy for dealing with the problem. He said he would use his newspaper and television connections to "blow the bastard out of the water" and in the process he likely would generate sales of ten thousand additional copies of "the book the Bronfmans could not suppress."

Kane urged the volatile Gray not to go public with the story while there was still the possibility a boycott could be avoided. "I can well understand how irritated you must be by the attempts to suppress *Booze*, but I really believe we must play this one cool until we have evidence of any attempts to interfere with our marketing plans," he wrote in a letter to Gray on 30 August 1972. "Let us agree, Jim, to hold our fire at least until further aggressive action occurs from the other side."

Gray backed down and agreed not to say anything to the media—at least for the moment—about a possible boycott. He sent off the marked galley proofs to Drache in Winnipeg, and felt vindicated when Drache said he did not think the younger generation of Bronfmans would find the material particularly offensive. "In fact, they would be very happy to have the founders pictured as being very robust guys from the wild and woolly West who stepped right into the big leagues and could trade punches with the best and come out on top." However, Drache acknowledged that some of the older generation might be disturbed by the references to the Bronfmans selling liquor to American bootleggers during the 1920s (although, in Canada, this had been a perfectly legal activity), and so he suggested that Gray might consider "toning down" some of these references to appease Vineberg. Gray changed about a dozen references as suggested by Drache, and was relieved when word came back from Vineberg that he was satisfied with the changes and had no further objections. *Booze* was then published on schedule, Classic Books ordered five hundred copies, and nothing about the threatened boycott ever appeared in the media.

The Toronto launch party for *Booze*—dubbed "the Boozerama" —was scheduled for 20 November 1972, a Monday, at the Butcher's Arms, a one-time nineteenth-century Jarvis Street bootlegging joint that had been recently converted into a high-end pub. (It was later closed due to financial problems.) Macmillan promotions director Nora Clark told Gray she was hoping to have the party on the Sunday before he started his two-day round of newspaper, radio, and television interviews. "However, Toronto is still under the influence of Prohibition, because liquor cannot be served on Sunday unless it is with a full dinner." Clark had also looked into the possibility of sending out small bottles of liquor with review copies of *Booze*, but scrapped that idea when she learned that Macmillan could be fined twenty-five thousand dollars by the Ontario licensing authorities for using liquor as a promotional device. Instead, she mailed empty liquor bottles to her media contacts.

By 27 November 1972, *Booze* was sitting at number seven on the *Toronto Star*'s national bestseller list, sales across the country had reached 9,262, and the positive reviews were arriving daily. "Gray's story of the Bronfmans is fascinating," William French wrote in *The Globe and Mail*. "He deserves full marks for digging up the facts, which were not always easily accessible." The University of Toronto's Michael Bliss would observe later that Gray's central argument in *Booze*—that Prohibition had worked in Canada—was "one of the most important insights that any historian ever had about Prohibition." It was an extraordinary example of Gray's ability to go to the heart of issues and ask important questions.

Nobody was happier about the early success of *Booze* than retiring Macmillan president John Morgan Gray. In a farewell letter to the author, he marvelled at how well Gray had done as a writer of books since Macmillan published his first book in 1966:

> Your story will always be for me one of the most interesting and attractive of all the publishing stories I know. Since you went back at *The Winter Years*, almost at retirement age, you have produced four further books. All entertaining, all valuable, and all, at least relatively, successful.
>
> Many writers starting much younger have achieved a good deal less. It raises a fascinating but unanswerable question: If we had published *The Winter Years* twenty-five years ago, what would have followed? Would there have been many more books, or did we merely tap a pool of creative energy that would have accomplished in twenty-five years what your pent-up frustration has given us in five or six?
>
> There's no answer, and fortunately there doesn't need to be. If you had not got in touch [in October 1962], I would have gone to my grave wondering about you and your book. But thank God I don't have to.
>
> I'm sure I have said this sort of thing to you before. And I hope you know that we realize none of it would have happened without great gifts added to immense energy and determination. If it adds up to a sense of great satisfaction, I hope you relax and enjoy it. It is yours by right.

Gray replied that he realized with hindsight that Macmillan

had been right not to publish the first version of *The Winter Years* in 1947: "The times were not right for a book on the Depression then. Everybody was much too close to it." Plus, he had a few more years of life experiences to pack in before he could write the kinds of books that would appeal to a general readership:

> I think the qualities that have made my books were in part the distillation of my Calgary as well as Winnipeg experiences. And, of course, the success which has been theirs has been the greatest experience of my life. And somehow or other I am sure that nothing that has happened would have come about if the first manuscript had been published or if I had in the end dealt with any other publisher. I guess you might say we were made for each other, and I am very happy this was so.

Maria and Harry Gray, Jimmie's parents, outside their Galt, Ontario, home, circa 1933.

Jimmie, age six, and brother Walter, age three, 1912.

Brothers (L to R)
Robert, age four,
Walter, age seven,
and Jimmie, age ten,
1916

Jimmie's youngest
brother, Robert, circa
1920.

Jimmie on his seventeenth birthday, during his first day of work at the Winnipeg Grain Exchange, August 1923.

First photo taken of Jimmie and Kay after their wedding in December 1926.

Kay and Jimmie and five-year-old daughter Patricia outside their Winnipeg home, 1933.

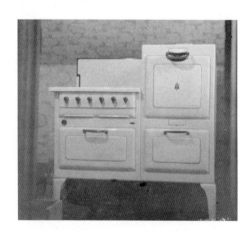

The electric stove Jimmie bought for five dollars down and five dollars a month after he came off unemployment relief in 1934.

Film actor Leslie Howard (wearing hat) visits the Winnipeg Free Press *newsroom in 1941 during the shooting of the movie 49th Parallel. Others in the photo are (L to R) editorial assistant Lucille Caldwell, columnist James H. Gray, city editor Howard Wolfe (seated), and managing editor Abbie Coo. (Nick Morant photo)*

Winnipeg Free Press *reporters try frying an egg on the sidewalk during the Manitoba heat wave of 1937. Pictured are (L to R) James H. Gray, Albert Booth, Jeff Hurley, and Earle Beattie. (Nick Morant photo)*

James GRAY ↓   J.W. DAFOE ↓

above: James H. Gray (wearing hat, left) and John W. Dafoe, editor-in-chief of the Winnipeg Free Press *(wearing hat, right), pictured outside the* Free Press *building, 1942. (* Winnipeg Free Press *photo)*

right: Kay and Jimmie, eight-year-old daughter Linda and ten-year-old son Alan, at Grasmere Farm, 1950.

*above: Jimmie (R)
and sixteen-year-old
daughter Pat social-
izing at New York's
Stork Club with two
of Gray's friends
who wrote for*
Newsweek *maga-
zine, July 1944.*

*left: Kay and Jimmie
at their daughter
Patricia's house in
Calgary, 1951.
Perky is the wire-
haired terrier in
front.*

right: "I'd Rather Be a Farmer." James H. at the microphone recording his weekly CFCN *radio program, 1952. (*CFCN *photo)*

below: Grasmere Farm, 1953.

Caricature of James H. attending the Pipeline Association of Canada conference at Castle Harbour Hotel, Bermuda, February 1959.

Jimmie riding Halloka Gloria, 1951.

Jimmie riding Pletera at Grasmere Farm, 1969.

Dr. W. A. (Bill) Cochrane, University of Calgary president, congratulates James H. after presenting him with an honorary doctorate, June 1975.

Jimmie at his home office in Calgary, 1977.

Kay and Jimmie celebrate their fiftieth wedding anniversary at the Calgary Petroleum Club, December 1976.

right: Jimmie at Grasmere Farm, 1984.

below: Kay and James H. (seated front right) at the 1987 induction ceremony for the Alberta Order of Excellence. Also inducted that year was renowned Alberta soil scientist Dr. Fred Bentley (seated front, second from left).

left: James H. and fellow historian Grant MacEwan at a social event marking the publication of Gray's A Brand of its Own: The 100 Year History of the Calgary Exhibition and Stampede *in 1985.*

below: The illuminated scroll of the Alberta Order of Excellence presented to James H., signed by the Order chancellor, Lieutenant-Governor Helen Hunley, and the chair, Mr. Justice Howard Irving.

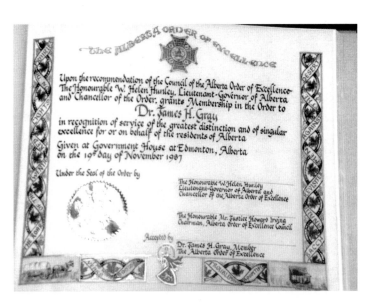

Governor General Jeanne Sauvé congratulates James H. after presenting him with the Order of Canada, November 1988.

James H. at the launch of his book Talk to My Lawyer! *in 1987. Also in the picture are Calgary lawyer John Martland and researcher Susie Sparks.*

above: Jimmie in his home office with the magnifying glass he used to help his failing eyesight, 1993.

left: James H. and Alderman Dave Bronconnier at the dedication of Calgary's James H. Gray Park, 1996.

right: Jimmie, son Alan, and daughter Patricia at the dedication of Calgary's James H. Gray Park, 1996.

below: James H. receiving the Canada National History Society's Pierre Berton Award from former prime minister Joe Clark, 1995.

Cracking the
American Market
1973-1979

The New American Library paperback edition of *Red Lights on the Prairies* brought James H. Gray his first major exposure in the United States, with more than 350,000 copies being offered on sale in American drugstores and corner groceries by June 1973. The US publisher did not expect, however, that all of these books would eventually wind up in the homes of American readers. As Hugh Kane of Macmillan pointed out, up to 40 percent of the distributed books were expected to come back to Canada unsold because of a returns policy—standard in the book industry—that allowed retailers to take books on consignment and return unsold copies for full credit. "But that still means the book is going to be bought and read by 210,000 new readers who would probably never buy the hardcover edition," Kane wrote in a letter to Gray on 14 June. "This is going to get you a vastly greater audience than you have ever had before. And your share of paperback royalties should amount to more than $10,000. That ain't hay, Jimmie!"

Gray was not impressed. "There is more to this paperback thing than money," he retorted. "The *Red Lights* paperback is a fraud of the worst order for it was designed to con the Americans into thinking they will be buying something of the *Happy Hooker* genre. I find myself repelled by the whole dirty business. If I needed the money, it would be different. But I've got more money now than I will ever spend, and I'd rather be remembered as a person who tried to do his best to arouse the interest of his countrymen in his country than as a fast-buck artist who would lend his name to anything as tawdry as this sort of promotion."

Gray's main complaint about the paperback edition of *Red Lights* was that the young women depicted on the front cover looked like high-class call girls, and thus bore no resemblance to the homely Prairie prostitutes whose pictures he had seen in police mug-shot files while doing his research. With a New American Library paperback edition of *Booze* also due to hit the American market, Gray worried that his honest studies of Canadian regional history were being distorted to appeal to a mass audience. Kane tried to argue that the book cover was merely a selling tool and that the integrity of Gray's work was preserved in the text of the paperback editions. But he soon realized that he was fighting a losing battle with the angry author, and so he backed down. "They are your books, so you're the boss," he wrote to Gray on 25 July 1973. "I have circulated your letter to everyone concerned, and we will make sure that no further work of yours appears in paperback after our present contractual obligations are discharged."

After this exchange, Gray decided that Macmillan might not be acting in his best interests when it came to negotiating paperback deals with the Americans. He was particularly upset when he discovered that Macmillan was pocketing 50 percent of the royalties paid by New American Library—a split that Kane said was "traditional in North American publishing, and accepted as fair and justifiable by most authors and literary agents." For this and for other reasons—including his feeling that Macmillan's book distribution system was no longer serving his interests—Gray agreed to join forces with his Canadian book-writing colleagues when novelist Margaret Laurence phoned him in August 1973. She invited him to become a member of a new national authors' group established to address concerns around such issues as foreign ownership of Canadian publishing houses and the importation by Canadian booksellers of cut-rate American overruns of Canadian books.

This new group was called The Writers' Union of Canada (TWUC) and it came into being to deal with the practical realities of being a professional book writer in Canada. Its mandate was to be conspicuously public, bringing the concerns of writers to the attention of governments, the media, the publishing industry, and the bookselling industry. (Pierre Berton insisted on having the word "union" in the name to establish its serious intent and set it apart from the fifty-year-old Canadian Authors Association, a collegial club of writing enthusiasts that granted membership to unpublished writers and teachers, as well as established book writers.) The founding TWUC members included such top Canadian authors as Margaret Atwood, Graeme Gibson, June Callwood, and Marian Engel. The founding executive director was Edinburgh-born arts administrator Alma Lee, who later established the Vancouver International Writers and Readers Festival and ran it successfully for seventeen years. Among TWUC's early initiatives was a picket demonstration outside a Coles bookstore in Toronto to protest the sale in Canada of remaindered American editions of books written by TWUC members while the more expensive Canadian editions were still on the shelves. The members discovered at the outset that a well-staged photo opportunity was one way to get the media to sit up and take notice.

Gray was pleased to be one of the eighty charter members of TWUC, who held their first get-together at Ottawa's National Arts Centre on 3 November 1973. For the previous nine years, he had made the writing of Canadian history his primary purpose in life—"my ongoing centennial project, if you will"—and yet the total royalties from his first three books had amounted to only twenty thousand dollars: less than half of what Ottawa classified as a poverty-level income in Canada. Gray felt there should be a better support system in place to assist Canadian writers financially. He did not need the money himself—he had his retirement income and his investments to sustain him—but he did think that others writing books about Canada for Canadians should be properly compensated by Canada for their efforts. "Does Canada owe every writer, every self-proclaimed poet a living?" he asked in a letter to Margaret Laurence. "Of course not. Canada owes nobody a living. But should not persons of demonstrable competence like myself be able to earn at least a minimum wage from our books? To that I say yes!"

Whenever TWUC was dealing with the practical concerns of writers, Gray was a willing and eager participant. He was front and centre in the early struggles to establish a system of payments to authors in recognition of the presence of their books in Canada's public and university libraries. He also fought to obtain compensation for authors for the photocopying of their works. "The problem of infringement of copyright through the mass use of photocopying is a very serious matter," he wrote in the TWUC newsletter. "We should canvass libraries and educational institutions to determine how many photocopying machines they have, and what safeguards are employed by the institutions to prevent wholesale pirating of copyright material."

Gray enjoyed attending TWUC's annual meetings in Ottawa and Toronto because it gave him a chance to sound off about issues that concerned him. The other members enjoyed his company because he had followed a different path to becoming an author. He came from a newspapering background and from the school of hard knocks, while they came from universities and creative writing schools. "The important stuff of the Union always happened in the bars after the meeting, and old James was great company at those gatherings—a very congenial fellow," author Andreas Schroeder would later recall:

> He would regale people. He had all these wild stories about whorehouses and juke joints, and he told them with the persona of a hard-drinking newspaperman who was also a

gentleman. He wouldn't tell you everything—he had a slight restraint that was appropriate to his own age and generation, and you would never hear him using explicit language. But it was always very clear what he was saying, and he did so in a delightfully reserved way. He convinced us that newspapermen always had the inside track, knew everything, and had sources for everything. If there was information to be gotten, Jimmie would have gotten it, and given it to you with great glee. He was a lovely man, no question about it.

Because there were fewer than one hundred Canadians earning the bulk of their income in the early 1970s from book writing and related activities, such as editing and public readings, TWUC had to broaden its membership base in order to grow. That meant offering memberships to writers who taught at universities or worked in libraries and bookstores. Gray viewed this development with some alarm, especially when the topics discussed at TWUC meetings shifted from the problems people encountered trying to make a living from writing to the state of Canadian literature and its place in the whole cultural scheme of things. "James didn't actually care about Canadian literature per se—he was really only interested in Canadian history—and he didn't much care about where literature fit into the cultural spectrum," said Schroeder, who was TWUC chairman in 1976-77. "Nor did he have much respect for a lot of university types. As more and more academics joined the Union, the nature and direction and tone of the organization changed a bit, and that annoyed James and made him realize that things were only going to get worse, not better. He could see it coming long before it arrived, and probably didn't see much future for himself in an organization of that sort. He was older than the rest of us by a fair way, and you could tell he would be leaving us sooner or later. He was a free spirit and he wasn't built for organizations with rules. But he did hang in for quite a few years, and he was a valuable founding member."

On 9 May 1977, Gray suggested in a letter to TWUC chairman Timothy Findley that the name of the organization be changed to "The Union of Canadian Novelists" because its concerns were for the problems of novelists "almost to the exclusion of problems affecting other branches of the writing craft." (In a letter to his CBC producer friend, Harry Boyle, Gray complained that the TWUC membership seemed to consist mainly of "lady novelists who fill their books with the words we used to write on bathroom walls as children.") However, as long as there were important battles to be won, Gray was still ready for the fray. In 1978, he took part in two notable and successful TWUC actions. When Pierre Berton announced that he planned to open an English-language book-store in downtown Montreal—"Take Me to Jail Bookstore"—to protest the Quebec law, Bill 101, requiring all advertising signs to be in French, Gray offered to volunteer as a helper at the store during his research trips to Montreal, and to goad the provincial government into having him arrested. (Quebec Premier René Lévesque subsequently bowed to public pressure and changed the law before the TWUC protest could proceed.)

The other TWUC initiative Gray took part in was the successful fight to get the federal government to stop Canadian book-sellers from importing and selling cheap American editions of Canadian books at a time when the original Canadian editions were still selling at full price. Gray had a special interest in this issue because the New American Library had overestimated the number of paperback copies of *Red Lights on the Prairies* that would sell in the United States and was dumping them back into the Canadian market. Instead of selling 210,000 copies as forecast by Hugh Kane, New American Library sold just 21,282 copies in the US during the first six months after its release, which at five cents a copy brought Gray royalties totalling $1,064.10.

Gray's final break with TWUC came in 1979, after six years of complaining that he had "heard more unadulterated crap at TWUC meetings than in a lifetime of auditing politicians," when the organization decided to increase the annual membership dues from a flat $120 to a sliding scale based on taxable income. The intent of the change was to help the union achieve independence from the Canada Council and Ontario Arts Council, which together provided half the union's operating revenue. The proposed scale ranged from $120 for writers whose taxable income was under $10,000 a year, up to $300 for those with a taxable income over $17,000. The point of contention for Gray was that TWUC members would be required to submit an accountant's statement as proof of income earned. He saw this as an invasion of privacy and an indication of lack of trust in the members, and he said so in a letter of resignation to TWUC chairwoman June Callwood on 22 May 1979.

Callwood appealed to Gray to stay with TWUC. "You are not only a respected writer, and a distinguished member of our profession, but you've also become, through longevity and personal qualifications, a Beloved Figure," she wrote on 5 July 1979. "We absolutely cannot spare you. We love you, don't go." But Gray's mind was made up. "I have no wish to continue an association with a group of people who operate on the principle that the membership cannot be trusted to tell the truth," he responded. "At my age, I have more pressing priorities for my time." Gray's resignation from TWUC came as no surprise to Schroeder. "Sooner or later, he was going to snag on something," he recalled. "James wasn't built to be a team member."

As it turned out, Gray was not the only member to resign from TWUC because of the new fee structure. Callwood reported in August 1979 that the union was in "mortal peril" because twenty-nine members had submitted letters of resignation and 180 more (half the entire membership) were refusing to pay their dues. The remaining TWUC members voted in October 1979 to jettison the contentious sliding scale, but by then Gray had moved on. Callwood appealed to him to "bless us with your continued support because you matter a great deal to us all." However, Gray replied that he could "probably advance the interest of Canadian writers better by going my own berserk way." In October 1980, Gray accepted an invitation to join the new Writers Guild of Alberta (WGA), a provincial organization similar to TWUC, but his involvement with that group ended before it even began. When the WGA voted at its founding meeting in Calgary to grant membership to anyone with an interest in writing, because it needed the numbers to get provincial government funding, Gray decided it was time for him to take a walk. "Too many amateurs," he snorted. "The Guild makes a farce of itself at its very first meeting."

The Roar of the Twenties
1975

James H. Gray was in no particular hurry to write another book after *Booze* was published in 1972. He was sixty-six years old, he had written five books about the history of the Prairies, and he was exhausted. "I am sure you recognize the feeling," he wrote in a letter to Bruce Hutchison, a fellow author and his former editor at the *Winnipeg Free Press*. "The writing, of course, is not the problem. It's the research and the endless hours of microfilm reading that did me in."

Through the course of writing his five books, Gray had established himself as the leading popular historian of the Canadian West. He was about to see the paperback edition of *Red Lights on the Prairies* released in the United States, and that would soon be followed by a paperback release of *Booze*. He had put Canadian history on the national bestseller lists, something only one other writer—Pierre Berton—had done during the same period. (Former *Vancouver Sun* columnist Barry Broadfoot would join them in 1973 with *Ten Lost Years*, a best-selling oral history of the Great Depression.) What else was there left for Gray to prove? Nothing, certainly, in terms of showing the book-buying public that the early Canadian West—while tamer than the American frontier—had a colour and flavour all its own.

But Gray still had plenty to say about his region and his

country, and as long as he had his trusty Smith Corona electric typewriter and a readership, he intended to say it. Ever the journalist, Gray spent part of every day firing off freelance articles, opinion pieces, and letters to the editors of newspapers and magazines. "You would be astounded at the number of things I get angry about," he told his daughter Pat. "That's why I write letters to the editor."

He also wrote letters to people with whom he had a beef of some kind. These could range from the governors of the Calgary Petroleum Club, whom Gray accused of denying membership to Jewish people (a charge they vehemently denied), to officials of Chrysler Canada, whom he soundly rebuked for building a Plymouth convertible with a roof he found impossible to fold back. After writing several letters demanding to know what kind of damage he would cause if he ignored the instructions in the driver's manual and left the back window zipped shut while lowering the top, Gray finally received a letter from an exasperated Chrysler vice-president saying that such "unapproved" action "could drastically affect the optical qualities of the rear window" and make the car dangerous to drive. Gray replied contemptuously that his next vehicle would likely be a Ford. (He was not kidding. In 1982, he abandoned Chrysler and bought himself a new Ford Mercury Cougar.)

Newspaper letters editors normally given to cutting down submissions for the sake of brevity invariably suspended their editing rules whenever Gray sent them a letter for possible publication. They saw that what he had to say was—as the letters editor of the *Calgary Herald* put it—"a matter of considerable public interest," and so they allowed him to ramble on for as long as he wanted. Sometimes it would be a matter of local public interest, such as the proliferation of American textbooks in Alberta schools and universities or the refusal by Calgary city council to restore the proper historic name to a stretch of municipal freeway traditionally known as the Old Banff Coach Road. Other times, it would be a matter of national concern, such as a 1973 proposal by the federal government to introduce tighter gun control legislation or what Gray perceived as a bias toward Quebec separatism in the writings of the Ottawa correspondents for Canada's English-language dailies.

His letters often contained a little history lesson for those who might not have read his books. When Calgary police chief Duke Kent told the provincial government in 1972 that his men should not be held legally responsible for policing rowdy behaviour in bars, Gray pointed out that Winnipeg's chief constable Christopher H. Newton had said the same thing in the 1920s, arguing that provincial laws, not city laws, were being broken. And when the minority Trudeau government in 1973 proposed a fence-mending conference between the federal and four western governments to find out what the West needed in terms of economic and social development, Gray suggested that Ottawa should have asked the same question in 1869 before trying to take control of the Red River Settlement in defiance of existing Métis occupancy.

In interviews with newspaper and magazine reporters after *Booze* was published, Gray said he planned to relax, enjoy his horses, do some travelling, spend time with his family, and leave the book writing to others. However, in what would become a recurring refrain over the next decade, Gray soon started saying that he had "one last book" to write before calling it quits. "There's been no good story of Western Canada in the Second World War years," he told *Quill and Quire* magazine in November 1972. "There's also another book about the Canadian railways that has to be written." He might also have added that there was a book to be written about the 1920s in western Canada because that's what he had in mind to write when he applied for a Canada Council grant in 1973 to do a book showing there was more to the post–First World War decade in the prairie provinces than the thirst for ebullient life depicted in American films and novels about the Jazz Age.

Gray outlined his proposal in a letter to Macmillan in June 1973. By this time, there was a new chain of upper command at the publishing company because the directors in London, England, had decided to sell off the Canadian arm when Toronto president John Morgan Gray announced his retirement. The new owner was Maclean-Hunter, a Toronto-based magazine publishing firm. Hugh Kane, John Gray's previously designated successor, was appointed president. However, Kane soon found himself reporting to a new CEO, George Gilmour, appointed by Maclean-Hunter with instructions to make book publishing as profitable as magazine publishing.

Gray, as a best-selling Macmillan author, had no problem persuading the new regime that he should do one more book for the publishing company. In a telephone conversation with editor Ken McVey, Gray said his proposed book about the 1920s would not give the readers a Great Gatsby, an Al Capone, or an Elliot Ness and the Untouchables. Instead, it would feature a collection of colourful Canadian characters, speculators, swindlers, and visionaries. And it would reveal some little-known facts. Did McVey know that a Winnipeg trade union newspaper called the *Bulletin* once achieved the largest circulation of any publication in Canada—more than 170,000 copies weekly—by giving away weekly prizes of ten thousand dollars in a betting pool on English soccer matches? (The paper folded after seven months when the Canadian courts declared the soccer pools illegal.) Or did he know that a former Ku Klux Klan organizer named D. C. Grant had helped a young socialist named Tommy Douglas get elected to his first term in Parliament in 1935? Or that a San Francisco lawyer named Aaron Sapiro—not a farm leader from Alberta or Saskatchewan—had inspired the cooperative movement that saw farmer-owned wheat marketing pools established throughout the Prairies? Or that the *Manitoba Free Press* had once chartered an aircraft to send its star reporter to the border town of Winkler, Manitoba, to cover a nineteen-thousand-dollar bank robbery that turned out to be the largest heist in the province's history? These were some of the stories Gray planned to tell in the book he would call *The Roar of the Twenties*.

The Canada Council awarded Gray a four-thousand-dollar

research grant in the fall of 1973, and he began the work of scouring the back files of the newspapers in Manitoba, Saskatchewan, and Alberta for potential story material. Though he already knew some of the stories he wanted to tell—such as the one about the Winnipeg cenotaph controversy that had earned him a letter of commendation from H. L. Mencken in 1934, and the story of how the liquor trade grew on the Prairies after Prohibition was repealed in the mid-1920s—Gray still felt he was venturing into what for him was largely unknown research territory. He worried constantly that he might be missing out on some news event that had engaged the attention of the entire prairie population, however briefly, during the decade. An example was the case of an American drifter and serial killer named Earle Nelson, who travelled through Manitoba and Saskatchewan in June 1927, strangled two women to death, and "brought on the greatest seizure of mass hysteria in all Prairie history." Gray rationalized that he might have been forgiven for missing this story because it had dropped off the national media radar during the time when Charles Lindbergh was receiving a hero's welcome in the United States for his historic trans-Atlantic solo flight. And it had been a story that began and ended quickly; the fugitive Nelson had been arrested and charged within ten days of his arrival in Canada. But still Gray worried that he might miss other, perhaps more important, regional stories and thus ruin his credibility as a prairie historian. "The research is most onerous and I am just about written out," he confided in a letter to his friend Jack Marshall of the *Windsor Star*. "Reading microfilm is a tedious and physically wearing chore. I confess to you that there have been several occasions when I have thrown up my hands and said, 'The hell with it.'"

A few months after starting his research, in December 1973, Gray received an invitation from the Winnipeg School Division that almost tempted him to put *The Roar of the Twenties* on permanent hold. Chief librarian Agnes L. Florence wrote to say that the school division wanted to establish a program stimulating an exchange of ideas between a successful author and the students, and wondered if Gray would be interested in becoming the division's first writer-in-residence for eight months. Gray wrote back to say that he was flattered by the invitation and was giving it serious thought, but he really did have an obligation to finish his 1920s book first. Instead, he told Florence he would be pleased to make presentations in the schools whenever he was in Winnipeg doing research for the book.

Gray thought of *The Roar of the Twenties* as essentially a memoir because much of it was drawn from his own memory of people and events. He had worked as a clerk at the Winnipeg Grain Exchange when high-rolling gamblers were winning and losing fortunes in the wheat market. He had owned shares in racehorses when a big-league huckster named Jim Speers was establishing a monopoly on racetrack gambling throughout Manitoba. He had been one of the "bootstrap boys" who clawed their way up from the bottom rung of the economic ladder to create a decent standard of living for themselves. And he had stood in the crowd outside the *Winnipeg Free Press* building on 4 July 1923, listening to an exuberant radio announcer relaying from the telegraph wires a blow-by-blow description of Jack Dempsey successfully defending his world heavyweight championship title against a little-known boxer named Tommy Gibbons in a fifteen-round bout at an outdoor stadium in Shelby, Montana. Yet for all of his personal involvement in the events of the decade, Gray chose to leave himself out of the book. He had already told of his 1920s experiences in *The Winter Years*, and so he turned *The Roar of the Twenties* into a detached, third-person chronicle of a time he remembered well.

Though he intended not to dwell much on politics in the book, because he wanted to focus on the things he saw as being more important in the lives of people during the 1920s—such as their work, their play, their home life, and their social interactions—Gray did make an exception in the case of the farmer-driven Progressive movement. He considered the reform-minded

Progressives to be important because they had played a vital role in the establishment of the wheat pools that revolutionized the commercial life of the West. They had been the first political party to give Canadian voters an alternative to the Liberals and the Conservatives at the federal level, and they also paved the way for the election of provincial farmer-run governments in Alberta and Manitoba. They were strongly affiliated with the United Farmers of Alberta when that party became the provincial government in 1921, and in 1922 they played a key role in the election victory of the Progressive Party of Manitoba.

Larger-than-life characters played key roles Gray's garrulous, gossipy book that appealed as much for its entertainment value as for its sober reflection on fact. The cast of characters included such distinctive Canadian con artists, millionaires, and gamblers as:

• Joseph Xavier Hearst, a ragtime pianist and songwriter ("You Can Take Me Away from Dixie but You Can't Take Dixie from Me") who tricked Manitobans into investing more than five hundred thousand dollars in a pyramid music publishing scheme that paid off early speculators with funds obtained from later victims.

• A. R. Davidson, a Winnipeg real estate tycoon who lived in a thirty-seven-room mansion that boasted the only passenger elevator in a house in western Canada and a railway-style turntable in the garage that allowed the chauffeur to avoid backing the family car in or out.

• Joe Auberge, a legendary Manitoba gambler who reportedly won and lost a paper fortune betting on wheat futures, ended up with a low-paying clerical job at the Winnipeg Grain Exchange, and was pointed out to visitors as he wandered the halls as a "great speculator who had ridden boom markets to disaster."

Gray also shone a light into some of the darker corners of prairie history during the 1920s. In one chapter, for instance, he wrote about the startling popularity of the Ku Klux Klan, which found new and fertile ground to till in Canada at a time when American states were systematically banning the secret society. In another chapter, sparing little in his description of prairie bigotry, he wrote about the quotas for Jewish students that were established and remained in place at the University of Manitoba's faculty of medicine until 1942.

Gray also wrote about the rise of the revolutionary western Canadian labour organization known as the "One Big Union," which ultimately failed because many of the workers wanted to eventually become their own bosses—not remain part of a movement that stood for radical socialism and the destruction of the capitalist system. A happier story of unity on the Prairies emerged from his description of the origins of the ecumenical movement that resulted in the formation of the United Church of Canada in 1925 by a union of Presbyterian, Methodist, Congregational, and Council of Local Union churches. Unlike the labour union, wrote Gray, the church union succeeded because it was already a *fait accompli* in rural communities across the Prairies. Parishioners often chose to attend churches more because of the local availability of Protestant pastors than because of sectarian conviction.

While to the casual browser *The Roar of the Twenties* might have seemed like a disparate collection of period essays linked only by the fact that the people mentioned in them had lived on the Prairies during the 1920s, there was one familiar subject—booze—that threaded its way into a number of the chapters. Gray had exorcized some of his personal demons by writing about his father's alcoholism in *The Boy from Winnipeg* and then by looking at the bigger picture of Prohibition-era alcohol use in *Booze*, but it seemed that he still had more to say on the subject. He began by speculating on how the history of the Bronfman family might have been different if the Senate had ratified a 1917 federal order-in-council forbidding the transportation of liquor into provinces where the sale of alcoholic beverages was outlawed because of Prohibition. By delaying the ratification order, the Senate opened the door for Harry Bronfman, then a hotel owner in Yorkton, Saskatchewan, to "found one of the great Canadian fortunes based upon the temporarily legalized interprovincial shipment of mail-order booze." Gray also traced a link between booze and the robberies committed on the Prairies during the 1920s. In border towns, especially, the bank robberies were carried out by American rum-runners who came across the border to buy liquor that could be legally supplied to them in Canada through distribution warehouses that Gray called "boozoriums." Gray even found a connection between booze and the emerging feminism movement on the Prairies during the 1920s. While the men were out drinking in the bars, the women—with their bobbed hair and short skirts—were at home either sipping prepared medicinal beverages with such names as Burdock's Blood Bitters and Lydia Pinkham's Vegetable Compound, or creating their own cocktails to make the harsh taste of alcohol more palatable.

Gray wrote the book piecemeal, researching and writing one chapter at a time before starting the research for the next chapter. On 12 March 1974, he wrote to Hugh Kane to say that this was not the most satisfactory way to write a book because he had no sense of the overall shape of the emerging manuscript and he thought the structure might be weak. "But it gets words on paper and ultimately the whole can be whipped into whatever shape is decided upon. My guess is that it will be completed come next New Year's Eve."

In June 1974, Gray took a break from researching and writing to travel to Winnipeg to accept an honorary doctorate of laws from the University of Manitoba. It was the first of three honorary degrees he would receive, and the great satisfaction it gave him can be gleaned from the passionate address he gave to the graduates at the convocation ceremony:

The most important and most relevant thing I can say to you is this: If Jimmie Gray could make it, anybody can make it. There is nothing any of you cannot do in this society of ours if you want to do it badly enough.

I can think of no place on Earth where somebody like me, with the tools I carried, would have been given the opportunity to do the things I have done. My appeal to you, in what is going to sound like a commercial for Canada, is that when you are deciding where your future lies, to give western Canada first chance. Whatever you want to be, whatever you want to do, my presence here today is all the assurance you need that you can make it here.

As a peaceful and compassionate community in which to bring up a family, this Prairie country is just about the best place of all. We are unique in that this is the only place in the world to which more than a million immigrants were lured in a single decade, and then dumped into an empty wilderness to live or die by their own exertions. No provision of any importance was made by any government to house, feed, succour, clothe or support them. Once they got here, there was no place else to go, and so they made the best of it. And it was out of this process of making the best of it that evolved the kind of society we have today. Whether they lived in the cities, towns or on homesteads, their survival required that the immigrants help one another. The legacy that comes down to us from our forefathers has been their willingness, their downright eagerness, to help one another. It is not a quality we talk much about, or are even conscious of. Yet we see it manifest everywhere in the social consciousness that permeates our governments and institutions. With such ancestors, it is no accident that Prairie people have long been leaders of movements for social reform, because social reform is only a high-blown synonym for helping one another.

As he had forecasted, Gray finished the first draft of *The Roar of the Twenties* by January 1975 and completed the revisions and rewrites over the next four months. By that time, the buzz in the book trade was that another potential Gray best-seller was about to hit the bookstands. Booksellers put in advance orders for four thousand copies—three hundred more than they had ordered of *Booze*—and two weekly magazine supplements that were distributed nationally in Canadian newspapers, *Weekend* and *The Canadian*, concluded deals with Macmillan to publish excerpts. *The Roar of the Twenties* appeared in bookstores on 23 May 1975 and was reviewed favourably in Canada's major newspapers, magazines, and academic journals. George Russell, writing in the Canadian edition of *Time* magazine, commented that Gray wrote "with a Menckenian disdain for the gullible and the academic." Carleton University's Wilfred Eggleston, writing in *The Beaver* magazine, described the book as a "vivid verbal cartoon." Doug Fetherling, in *Saturday Night* magazine, complimented Gray for writing with "wit, intelligence, and a careful attention to fascinating detail." The University of Calgary's David Bercuson, writing in *The Canadian Historical Review*, noted that Gray's love of western Canada and its people showed through in every chapter of his books. "Rumours abound that *The Roar of the Twenties* will be his last major work," wrote Bercuson. "But if James Gray keeps on loving his people, he'll keep on writing their history, and we'll all be richer for it."

Gray was pleased with the complimentary reviews, but he was now so convinced he would never do another book that he wrote a letter to this effect to the new Macmillan president, George Gilmour. "At the end of a book authoring career, I think it only fitting that I should say that I have never had an association I have enjoyed more than with the people at Macmillan," Gray began. He went on to list all the individuals he had worked with at Macmillan over the previous twenty years—presidents John Morgan Gray and Hugh Kane, editor Ken McVey, and publicist Nora Clark—and concluded by saying, "I think you have every reason for pride and confidence in the people who ride herd on your authors from first until last contacts. I felt it was about time that you had an author put that on permanent record."

Aside from the fact that he was tired of microfilm reading, Gray had another reason for thinking *The Roar of the Twenties* would be his last book. He was about to launch a one-person crusade that would keep him busy for the next few years—trying to get more Canadian history, especially prairie history, taught in the schools.

History in the Schools
1975-1977

Macmillan president Hugh Kane was clearly upset when James H. Gray announced in June 1975 that *The Roar of the Twenties* would be his last book. "There are still many aspects of Western Canadian history that need recording," Kane wrote in a letter on 23 June 1975, urging Gray to change his mind. But Gray's mind was made up, at least for the time being. He was going to do his bit to improve Alberta's education system by lobbying government to have more prairie history taught in the schools. That meant he would have no more time for writing books.

Gray had been interested in education ever since he was a seven-year-old sitting around the kitchen table with his parents, doing his homework while they practised their handwriting. Self-education had given him his passport to a writing career when he was on unemployment relief during the 1930s, and he had always wanted his children to do well in school. He was particularly pleased when his daughter Linda was able to skip grade one and start elementary school in grade two because she had learned the basics of reading while in kindergarten. When his son, Alan, scored low marks in mathematics in high school, Gray hired a math tutor to ensure he would get into university. And when his oldest daughter Pat began struggling in grade seven, Gray did not think she was applying herself sufficiently well to her studies and insisted that she

repeat the grade. Yet to show her that he also believed in reward-
ing scholastic achievement, Gray promised Pat that if she did well
in grade eleven, he would take her on a trip to New York City.

As it turned out, Pat did not obtain top marks in grade eleven.
But her father—after some nudging from Kay—took her to New
York City anyhow, in July 1944. Sixty years later, Pat would
remember the trip with great fondness. "He did a really wonderful
thing for me that I've always appreciated," she recalled. "He never
knew how much I got out of it." They took the train from
Winnipeg to Montreal, where they stayed with Clifford Sifton, a
member of the family that owned the *Winnipeg Free Press* and other
prairie newspapers, and spent the night on Sifton's boat. "For this
little girl from Winnipeg, that was fantastic," Pat said. Then they
flew to New York—Pat had never been on a plane before—where
they lunched at the Stork Club with two of Gray's journalist
friends from *Newsweek* magazine, walked through Harlem, visited
Coney Island, and went to see the Broadway musical *Oklahoma*.

With history being his primary focus as an author, Gray came
to believe that his children had not learned much about Canadian
history while in school and that later generations of schoolchild-
ren were not learning much about it either. The situation did not
seem to have improved much by 1975, after Gray had published six
books of prairie history, and so he started writing letters to Alberta
teachers and bureaucrats, urging them to add more Canadian history to the school curricula:

> The last decade has seen an unparallelled [sic] explosion of
> interest in Canadian history by Canadian writers. More superb
> works of Canadian history have been produced in this
> decade than in the previous 100 years of nationhood. Our
> writers have discovered abilities to make this country's his-
> tory as fascinating, as exciting as that of any people on Earth.
> The books they have produced have found delighted accept-
> ance by the over-fifty generation all across the country.

And they have gone unnoticed where acceptance is the most vital—in the lower reaches of our educational systems.

It has disturbed me greatly to discover that the young people of Alberta are emerging from high school in almost total ignorance of the history of Canada and of the province of Alberta. It was a shattering discovery for me to find there were young Canadians who know nothing of Canada's participation in two world wars. It was a worse experience, if that were possible, to discover they knew nothing of developments on these Prairies during the Great Depression which changed the face of world agriculture.

Our classrooms in Alberta today are the bailiwicks of earnest and conscientious young Bachelors of Education who came through our universities uncontaminated by exposure to national, regional or local history. Thirty years of university control in Alberta by the California educational mafia have brought us to the point where the teaching profession is dominated overwhelmingly by people who know little and care less about Canadian history. So they are impervious to the new waves of history washing over them, and they are not teaching it in the schools. We have to find a way of getting books about Canadian history into the hands of the coming generation so that they, by becoming aware of their Canadian heritage, can avoid the mistakes made by previous generations.

The teachers and the bureaucrats had no real quarrel with Gray's argument. They all agreed that it was important for students to know about the history of their region and their country. "The only trouble is that there are no useful texts available," he quoted them as saying to him. In that case, Gray replied, why does not the government sponsor a contest with "substantial cash prizes" given to those who write the best history textbooks for use in Alberta's schools? He thought each book could contain about sixty or seventy pages of text, and be filled with photographs to appeal to young people. Again, the bureaucrats agreed. Officials from the Department of Youth Culture and the Department of Education indicated to him that they were "a bit more than mildly interested." Despite this, however, they seemed to be in no hurry to act on his proposal. Looking on the positive side, Gray decided that this was just a typical instance of government mills grinding slowly, and that eventually he would be given the green light to organize a textbook writing contest. However, the government, as it turned out, had a different plan—an elaborate eight-million-dollar scheme—for adding more Canadian content to the schools' curricula. Gray would eventually be invited to participate in this as-yet-unpublicized project, but in the meantime, with nothing else to keep him busy, he decided to take up golf—a game he had not played since his brief foray into the miniature golf business in 1930.

With the same dedication he had once given to upgrading his education at the Winnipeg Public Library, Gray set out to master the game of Arnold Palmer and Jack Nicklaus. He practised pitching and putting during his annual February sojourn to California with Kay at the Monte Vista Hotel in Palm Springs, and hit a thousand balls on a Calgary driving range during the summer and fall of 1975. He told his pal Gorde Hunter, a retired sportswriter in Victoria, British Columbia, that he aimed to shoot an eighteen-hole round of ninety before his seventieth birthday on 31 August 1976. (The record does not show whether Gray actually achieved his golfing goal.)

Reaching his seventieth birthday was one important personal milestone for Gray in 1976. Celebrating his fiftieth wedding anniversary was another. He had always felt guilty about the fact that he and Kay never had a traditional church wedding or honeymoon, and so he was determined to make her golden anniversary a special event. He offered her the option of deciding where she would like to have the reception—at home or at a restaurant—and Kay immediately chose the Calgary Petroleum Club, where she had always enjoyed dining with Jimmie. In the summer of 1976, he booked the downtown club for a dinner on 28 December for up to seventy guests and—without saying anything to Kay—wrote a letter to the business agent for Juliette, a popular CBC television singer, asking if she would be available to sing some songs from the 1920s at the reception.

Juliette was not able to come to Calgary for the Gray anniversary celebration, but another Vancouver-based singer, Norma Locke, said she would be delighted to entertain at the event. Locke, the wife of dance bandleader Mart Kenney and the featured singer with Kenney's popular Western Gentlemen orchestra, said she would waive her performance fee if Gray covered airfare and hotel accommodation for herself and her husband. Gray agreed and Kay got to hear some of her favourite songs from the 1920s onward— "You Made Me Love You," "Bye Bye Blackbird," "Making Whoopee," "My Baby Just Cares for Me," "That Old Feeling, "Blue Moon," "Some of These Days," and "The Anniversary Waltz"— being performed live at the anniversary celebration. Kenney played clarinet during the gig and led the accompaniment by the Petroleum Club house band of trumpet, piano, bass, and drums.

The anniversary celebration was a great success. Jimmie was on his best behaviour, biting his tongue when he might have been tempted to complain loudly about the food or the service. He had often done this when dining at the Petroleum Club, reducing waitresses to tears because they had served the meal either too hot or too cold for his taste. However, on this occasion he had no complaints, and all agreed afterwards that it was a first-class affair. "It was lovely for Mom," Pat would recall. "So much happiness." Sam Drache, Jimmie's lawyer friend from Winnipeg, told the guests that a tree commemorating the Grays' anniversary would be planted in Canada Park, a wooded recreation area built with money provided by the Canadian Jewish National Fund in the Israeli-occupied West Bank. Jimmie touched many hearts when he presented Kay with an engraved gold ring and talked about the qualities she had brought to their relationship: "The serenity, and the equanimity that she brought to this marriage of ours made it possible for it to survive for fifty years when it had no licence whatever to survive for one year. I put this ring in your hand, Kay, and I say to you: If you would like to take another ride on this carousel of life with me, would you let me put this wedding ring on your finger on this 28th day of December, 1976?"

After the party was over, Jimmie started making arrangements to take Kay to the Monte Vista Hotel in Palm Springs, California, for their annual February break—something he had done every year for the previous ten years to escape the winter cold in Calgary. He advised his various correspondents that his phone would be disconnected while he was away and that he would not be answering any mail. When he returned to Calgary, he would be renewing his one-man crusade to get more Canadian history taught in the schools. However, when his winter vacation was over, Gray was ready once more to answer the call from Macmillan to write another book.

Selling the Farm
1977

When he worked as a journalist, James H. Gray always preferred to do his talking with his typewriter. As he explained in a September 1967 address to the Knights of the Round Table in Calgary, "I felt there was already an overabundance of dull speeches being delivered without me adding to the general boredom of the listening audience." Once he became a published author, however, he had to resign himself to the reality that speaking in public was part of the book marketing process. "My publisher, the Macmillan Company of Canada, has told me that my career as a non-speaker is over," he told the Knights. "From now on, I am expected to get out on the rubber-chicken circuit, and harangue with my comments whatever multitude is there assembled. The idea, of course, is that in this way we will drum up some extra sales for my book."

Sometimes his speeches made the news. Gray had a clever way of extracting material from his published writings to offer a view of Canadian history that seemed fresh and new to those who had not studied the subject. So, for example, when he talked about the impact of the Great Depression on the farmers of the Prairies, he portrayed it not as the conventional saga of unrelieved poverty, drought, and misery, but as a great opportunity that presented itself when scientists and farmers got together to fight the destructive forces of nature and develop new agricultural techniques. And when he talked about the aftermath of the Depression, instead of echoing the standard line of western provincial politicians who blamed the eastern banks for destroying the western economy, he opted instead to look at the positive and praise the federal government for introducing such beneficial social programs as family allowances, unemployment insurance, and improved old-age pensions.

Normally when Gray's speeches made the news, they received coverage only in the local newspapers. However, in June 1977, he gave a speech that won heavy coverage in the national media—the first speech to use the term "New Canada" and the word "maverick" to define the place of the prairie provinces in Confederation. Long before Reform Party leader Preston Manning used the term "New Canada" to describe his vision of Canada in the twenty-first century, and long before author Aritha van Herk chose the word "mavericks" as the title of a best-selling popular history of Alberta, Gray was using the words in a speech in Toronto about the future of Confederation.

He gave the speech at a conference called Destiny Canada, organized by Toronto's York University in the wake of the November 1976 Quebec election that saw the sovereigntist Parti Québécois rise to power. The conference, billed by organizers as a national "town hall meeting," with invitations sent to hundreds of people from different segments of Canadian society, was to focus on the things Canadians would have to do to build a stronger and more unified country. Gray was one of seven keynote speakers at the conference. The others included former Ontario Premier John Robarts, soon-to-be Quebec Liberal leader Claude Ryan, CBC broadcaster Barbara Frum, historian Ramsay Cook, economist William Jenkins, and journalist Solange Chaput-Rolland. The event was covered by more than two hundred reporters—a contingent described by *Globe and Mail* writer Arnold Bruner as "about the size of the press turnout for some small wars."

Gray was invited to appear as a spokesman for "the West," and in his opening remarks to the 450 delegates he said that they should immediately disabuse themselves of the notion that the West actually existed as a homogenous cultural entity: "There are three Prairie provinces and British Columbia—which is a world all its own," he said. "A much better term for our part of the country would be New Canada. And the part of the New Canada turf that I have staked out for myself is the Great Plains country east of the Rockies." Inattention on the part of "Old Canada" was the main obstacle to New Canada's development as a strong partner in Confederation, Gray said. Central Canada's myopic view of western Canada as simply a geographic and cultural extension of Quebec and Ontario betrayed a "woeful ignorance" of the nature and history of the region. "New Canada is not a branch growing out of the main trunk of Central Canada," he said. "It's a separate and distinct variety that has been grafted on the Central Canada root stock."

Gray noted that at the time of Confederation in 1867, there were three million people of European origin in central Canada, two million who spoke English and one million who spoke French. At that time, New Canada was populated by five million buffalo, about fifty-five thousand Natives and Métis, and less than two thousand settlers of European origin. The main settlement of these "empty" prairies occurred after the Métis dispersed and the Natives had been confined to reserves comprising less than 1 percent of the region's total area. Between 1896 and 1911, more than one million people came into the region to—as Gray put it— "graft a new branch onto the Canadian tree." They came in equal numbers from the British Isles, central and eastern Europe, and— because the American frontier had been officially closed to settlers in 1890—from the United States. In fact, so many settlers came up from the States—more than three hundred thousand in all—that the American government campaigned to stop them from leaving by propagandizing about the harshness of Canadian winters and the "peculiarities" of the British system of government.

Not all of the Americans who came to the Prairies were American-born, Gray noted. Many hailed originally from Britain, Germany, Ukraine, Austria, Poland, and other parts of Europe. They came to Canada after first trying to establish themselves in the United States, and brought with them the values and attitudes of their transitional homeland. Thus, unlike in Quebec and other parts of French-speaking Canada, where two solitudes grappled with the problem of trying to share a single country, the immigrants of New Canada blended together in a melting pot where concerns about language rights were almost nonexistent. "What we are seeing now is the flowering of a new people," Gray said. "We are a maverick people, conscious of our own strength, and of the important role we can play in the Canadian scheme of things—if we can only get Central Canada to listen."

Central Canada, as it turned out, was listening—if only for that particular weekend. When Gray offered a tongue-in-cheek prescription for making the Canadian Broadcasting Corporation's "national news" live up to its name by not running any American news and by including stories from the front pages of at least five major western dailies, he found an unlikely ally in broadcaster Barbara Frum, then the host of CBC Radio's phone-out program, *As It Happens*. In what seemed like a mischievous attempt to bite the hand that fed her, Frum told the conference delegates that the CBC was like Canada itself—dysfunctional and deeply divided, with separate English and French components, "neither of which knows anything about the other." If one wanted to find a "working model of how Canada will fail," Frum said, one should look no further than the CBC.

Frum's comments made the front page in the next day's *Globe and Mail*, and Gray's remarks were included as part of the story. His speech was also covered by the *Montreal Star* and by *Maclean's* magazine. However, Gray was characteristically unimpressed by this attention from the eastern media. "If I'd made the same speech out here," he told a reporter for *St. John's Calgary Report*, "nobody down there would have heard of it at all." When a tree fell in Toronto, the sound ricocheted from coast to coast, he said. When a tree fell in Calgary, nobody in Toronto cared.

Gray's speech at the Destiny Canada conference brought him a fan letter from future Reform Party leader Preston Manning, then a thirty-five-year-old management consultant working in the Alberta oil and gas industry. Manning thanked Gray for underlining central Canada's narrow view of western Canada as an extension of Ontario and Quebec, and suggested that Gray might be just the person to "trigger the explosion it will take to knock this misconception out of the minds of the academic and political elites of Central Canada."

However, as tempted as he might have been to follow up on Manning's suggestion and go on a speaking tour to educate easterners about the realities of western Canada, Gray opted instead to remain in Calgary to take care of a domestic issue. For some time he had been concerned about the fact that Grasmere Farm, his country home on the northwest outskirts of Calgary, was being threatened by encroaching development. Now, in the summer of 1977, he had an opportunity to sell the twenty-acre property to Calgary land developer Gordon Donaldson for $525,000. "At last we have found an answer to the question, what shall we do with our land?" he wrote in a letter to his son, Alan, and daughter Linda. "It is one that has been troubling us off and on for several years. It has made living with uncertainty an unsettling sort of existence. Now it is settled and we can go on from here." Linda was saddened to learn that the family home where she had spent ten happy years of her young life was to be demolished, but she could understand her father's reasoning. His rural neighbours had been subdividing their properties as the city expanded toward the west and north, and so he had known for some time that development in his neighbourhood was inevitable. "If we had not made this deal, we would have risked being hemmed in by construction in a manner which might have substantially reduced the value of our land," he said.

Gray's plan was to buy a custom-built house for about $130,000 in one of the new subdivisions being developed in the south-western quadrant of Calgary now encompassing Patterson Heights, Prominence Point, Coach Hill, and Strathcona Park. He would give Kay half of the three hundred thousand dollars left in his bank account after he had paid seventy-five thousand dollars in capital gains tax on the sale of Grasmere Farm and given cash gifts to each of his three children. He would then encourage Kay to take charge of her own finances. Kay, then aged seventy-five, had been concerned for some time about her older brother Tommy—a dementia sufferer—and she worried that she might be stricken with a similar condition. Gray decided that one way to forestall this possibility was to have Kay open a separate bank account, start reading the financial pages, and take responsibility for managing her own money. By so doing, she would exercise her brain "and not turn into a vegetable like her brother."

As it turned out—though the family did not realize it yet—Kay was already in the early stages of mental decline when she and Jimmie moved in 1980 to their new home in Strathcona Park, a couple of kilometres south of Grasmere. She betrayed absolutely no emotion when Jimmie gave away his remaining two horses, Stormy and Pletera, to friends Lenore and Stan Wilson, nor when she saw the bulldozers coming to demolish the country home she had shared with Jimmie for twenty-seven years. The shadows were beginning to lengthen on Kay's front lawn by that time and would only lengthen further in the years to come.

Troublemaker!
1977-1978

Hugh Kane resigned as president of the Macmillan Company of Canada in September 1976 to take a pre-retirement job with a subsidiary of McClelland & Stewart. At age sixty-five, he no longer had the energy or desire to turn Macmillan into the profit centre demanded by his new bosses at Maclean-Hunter. As author Roy MacSkimming characterized him in *The Perilous Trade: Publishing Canada's Writers*, Kane was "an old-fashioned bookman, not up to Maclean-Hunter's notion of an efficient modern executive, and he had actively campaigned against its takeover offer." His responsibilities as president were assumed by Macmillan CEO George Gilmour.

Gilmour and Doug Gibson—the latter a Scottish-born trade editor who had been recruited from Doubleday Canada in 1974 to assume the position of editorial director of Macmillan's trade division—kept urging James H. Gray to write one more book, and in April 1977 Gray finally relented. His efforts to put Canadian history into the school system had stalled, the golfing was only keeping him occupied sporadically between the months of May and October, and he actually did have another book project in mind. Gray told Gibson it would be a chronological sequel to *The Winter Years*, tracking social developments on the Prairies from the time he started working for the *Free Press* in 1935 to the time in 1958 when he had joined Home Oil to promote president Bobby Brown's proposal to build a pipeline to carry Alberta crude oil to refineries in Montreal.

Gray completed a sample chapter—about his McCarthyist experience at the *Winnipeg Free Press* in 1937 when he was falsely accused of being a communist sympathizer—and sent it off to Macmillan executive editor Ken McVey in August 1977 along with a letter outlining what else he planned to include in the book. He had chosen the title, "Testament," "tentatively, because there is probably a better one lying around," and said the book would follow the pattern established in his previous books, "where it happened to me, or I was there when it happened." One chapter would deal with his career at the *Farm and Ranch Review*. Another would deal with his fight to keep the *Western Oil Examiner* afloat in the face of an advertising boycott by US oil company executives who "accused me of being an anti-American son-of-a-bitch." Additionally, there would be chapters on the impact of the Second World War on western Canada, Gray's career as an Ottawa correspondent, and what he called "the war of the Dafoe succession"— which took place when *Free Press* publisher Victor Sifton gave the editor-in-chief's job to a troika of senior newsroom employees following the death of John W. Dafoe on 9 January 1944. "So," he asked McVey, "the question before the House is: If you have half a dozen chapters similar to the enclosed, do you have a book?"

McVey replied on 17 August 1977 that he was sure there was a book in Gray's proposal, "and a damn good one, as usual." He did not like the suggested title of "Testament"—"it sounds a bit somber to me"—but he was sure they could find a better title as the manuscript developed. Then, a month later, McVey dropped a bombshell. He told Gray he would be leaving Macmillan in October 1977 to take a job as a literary consultant with the Alberta government's Department of Culture. Gray expressed his shock in a letter to Gibson on 25 October 1977:

The news that Ken McVey is leaving Macmillan will be regarded by your authors as little short of the second coming of the Titanic. I speak with some feeling because it takes one to know one. I am an old copy editor myself. I know what a dismal task it can be to pore over somebody else's less than deathless prose. So, far more than any of your authors, I have an appreciation of what a superb craftsman Ken was and is.

In the four of my books he has handled, I cannot think of a single suggestion Ken made which was not an improvement on what I had done. In addition, when I have written my way into a corner, and found myself spinning around in circles with no way out, he has been able to come up with a solution which was always embarrassingly simple and very much to the point. For myself, his leaving will give me just a hell of a good excuse for getting out of the book-writing business.

Because McVey had spent the previous nine years working as Gray's editor, and because he was already corresponding back and forth with Gray about his latest book project, he asked for and received permission from his new bosses at Alberta Culture to let him see the book project through to completion. Gray was pleased with this turn of events, and by December 1977 he and McVey had agreed on what the title of the book should be: "In as much as it is largely about the trouble I have made, I think we should call it *Troublemaker!*" (The full title, when published, was *Troublemaker!: A Fighting Journalist's Personal Record of the Two Booming Decades that Followed The Winter Years*.)

In writing the book, Gray saw himself as following in the footsteps of Vincent Sheean, a revolutionary American journalist who had gone to the Soviet Union in 1926 to report on the unfolding of Bolshevism and had then changed, in Gray's words, "from objective reporter to inflamed zealot—a partisan polemicist in the intellectual controversies that enveloped his subject." Gray, too, saw himself as someone who had evolved from objective reporter at the *Free Press* into a rabble-rousing commentator at the *Farm and Ranch Review* and *Western Oil Examiner* who "became caught up in the currents that were changing the face of western Canada and became a partisan shouter against the tide."

If people had read *The Roar of the Twenties*, in which Gray breathlessly declared that the 1920s was the West's most exciting decade, "more exciting than anything that happened anywhere else in the country," and then read his introduction to *Troublemaker!*, in which he maintained with equal conviction that the period between 1935 and the mid-1950s was "the most exciting, most elevating, most critical and most illuminating two decades in Prairie history," they might have wondered which of these sweeping conclusions was correct. They would likely have concluded that University of Calgary historian David Bercuson was probably exaggerating only slightly when he wrote in *The Canadian Historical Review* in March 1977 that academic historians always kept a ten-foot pole handy to jab at Gray's inconsistencies. But Gray was only doing what he had learned during his twenty years as a journalist, and that was to grab the readers by the lapels and never let them go. In his mind's eye, there was always a big sign hanging over his desk—similar to one that a *New York Journal* managing editor, Arthur Brisbane, is said to have insisted on having installed in his newsroom—that said, in letters one metre high, "They Don't Want to Read It!" Gray was not writing for the academics, he was writing for the people who believed—as he did—that great benefits had always accrued to those who lived on the Prairies, even during droughts and depressions and other disasters. He was writing for the people who shared his conviction that the Prairies had always been populated by optimists. And if that meant having to indulge in a bit of media-style exaggeration, so be it. Nobody could ever accuse James H. Gray of having his heart in the wrong place.

In *Troublemaker!*, Gray offered a personal view of life on the Prairies as seen first from the newsroom of the *Winnipeg Free Press*, and then from the other journalistic pews that he occupied between the 1930s and the 1950s. Discursive, opinionated, dialogue-driven, and relentlessly honest despite the occasional lapse into hyperbole, the book roamed back and forth across the decades. It covered events in which Gray had played a role as participant or observer, and ignored some stories—even major stories such as the ones about the massive wartime initiative known as the British Commonwealth Air Training Plan and the forced resettlement of Japanese-Canadians after Pearl Harbor—that had taken place while he was distracted by other things.

In one chapter of the book, Gray told how he tried to make amends after writing an opinion piece for the *Winnipeg Free Press* in which he accused the promoters of an Alberta oil drilling venture of offering potential investors a dubious form of share involvement known as royalty financing. Gray considered himself to be an expert on stock market fraud after having worked at the Lethbridge office of disgraced mining broker Isaac Solloway in 1929, and he viewed the promises of Turner Valley Royalties with great suspicion. He noted that instead of offering standard variable-yield shares to investors, the company was promising a fixed royalty-like percentage of the income earned by a well if it struck oil. Gray saw this as a highly risky proposition for the investors. He said so in a column he wrote in the spring of 1937 and found himself being accused of libelling the industry. A Winnipeg stockbroker named Alex Freeman took him to task and supplied charts, production figures, and royalty statements to show that—far from running a swindle—Turner Valley Royalties was actually offering a revolutionary form of oil well investment that virtually guaranteed a high return to investors. After scrutinizing Freeman's file on the Alberta company—which happened to be co-owned by Bobby Brown's father—Gray wrote a follow-up, *mea culpa* piece for the *Free Press* in which he said that the royalty system of financing was so effective that it should also be used for mining and other industries.

Gray covered some big economic topics in *Troublemaker!*—like wartime rationing and wage and price controls—and put a human face on them by relating them to events in his own life. In 1946, he had learned about the brisk post-war trade in used cars of questionable standard when he decided he needed a vehicle to get around Ottawa while covering stories for the *Free Press*. In Winnipeg, during the war, he had travelled to work by streetcar. Even if he had wanted to buy a car, he would have been unable to do so because of the government's wartime ban on automobile sales for civilian use. In Ottawa, after the war, he felt he could not live without wheels. He grabbed the *Ottawa Journal* every day as soon as it hit the streets, hoping to get the jump on others scouring the advertisements for the best car deals. When he finally found what seemed like a suitable vehicle—a ten-year-old Buick sedan with two well-treaded spare tires—he felt confident that he had made a good $1,200 purchase because the seller was an RCMP constable. However, when he took the car to a mechanic to check out a rattling noise under the hood, he discovered that even the Mounties were not to be trusted when it came to dealing in used cars. The front coil springs were held together with haywire and clearly beyond repair. Gray tried to take the vehicle back to the Mountie for a refund, but the officer had already used the money to pay off his car loan. That left Gray with no choice but to put an ad in the paper, sell the car to the first person who rang his doorbell, and hope the buyer would not be back the following day looking for a refund.

Gray's second attempt to buy a car in Ottawa was no more successful than the first. This time the seller was a Member of Parliament from Manitoba, who insisted that Gray would have to pay him the going black-market price if he wanted something more dependable than a lemon bound together with haywire. It was not until Gray enlisted the help of his brother Walter—who ran a lumberyard in Cambridge (formerly Galt), Ontario, and was owed a favour by a local car dealer—that Gray was able to get a reliable vehicle without having to pay through the nose for it.

In June 1978, Gray completed his chronicle of his adventures in the used-car trade and his account of his experiences in the newspaper business during the "two booming decades that followed *The Winter Years*." Gibson and Macmillan managing editor Jan Walter both congratulated him on a job well done. "We're delighted with what Ken [McVey] and you have done with the manuscript," said Gibson. "It reads well and should sell well." Walter—a recent addition to the Macmillan editorial team following stints with Hurtig Publishers and Fifth Business Books in Edmonton—told Gray that *Troublemaker!* had received an enthusiastic welcome from the staff during Macmillan's weekly sales meeting. "It was the first title presented and, as expected, the promise of another Gray bestseller soon warmed up the house."

The book was published in November 1978 and Gray, crusty as ever, was not pleased with the production job done on it. He complained to Jan Walter that the mimeographed reproductions of the editorials he had written for the *Farm and Ranch Review* and *Western Oil Examiner* were unreadable, and said that he hated the dust jacket, which featured a grainy photo of Gray as a young reporter, dapper in a dark suit and fedora. However, he kept his complaints to himself when talking to the news media about the book. During an interview with Fraser Perry of *The Albertan* newspaper, he pointed to his picture on the cover, grinned, and said, "Howard Hughes."

The reviewers were clearly pleased to see that Gray had again postponed his planned retirement from book writing. Peter C. Newman, writing in *Maclean's* magazine, said *Troublemaker!* was "not just well-researched history-on-the-hoof. It's damn fine reading." Jamie Portman, national arts correspondent for the Southam newspaper chain, described it as "a book of great immediacy and appeal—warm-hearted, wise and extraordinarily revealing about ourselves." Doug Fisher, writing in the *Toronto Sun*, characterized Gray as a "distinctive yet well-matched complement to the better known Pierre Berton in the East. Strong personalities, popular historians, each is a great exponent of what I sense is Canada." Other reviewers criticized Gray for casting himself as the leading character in many of the stories covered in the book, and for writing in what Peter Quince in *Western Living* magazine called a "newspaperman's fervid style." But on the whole the reviewers recommended it as a book that all Canadians should read. Editor Cleo Mowers wrote in the *Lethbridge Herald*: "For those who want to understand the background of today's foreign domination of the Canadian oil industry or the background of today's national press, this book is required reading."

Troublemaker! was Gray's last book for Macmillan. In 1979, Maclean-Hunter chairman Donald Campbell decided to unload the seventy-four-year-old publishing house after concluding it was too small to be profitable. The new owner was Gage Educational Publishing of Chicago (later Gage Learning Corporation, and after that, Thomson Nelson), which completed the takeover for a reported $3 million in July 1980. Gage president Ron Besse, a Canadian who had previously served as the president of McGraw-Hill Ryerson, said at first that the entire Macmillan backlist—which included titles by such authors as Hugh MacLennan, Morley Callaghan, Stephen Leacock, Robertson Davies, Alice Munro, Mavis Gallant, and Carol Shields—would remain in print. Doug Gibson, newly appointed by Besse as publisher of the Macmillan trade list, assured the authors at a Toronto media conference in December 1980 that if they felt at home at the "old" Macmillan, "you'll feel at home at the new Macmillan."

Less than a month after the 1980 Toronto news conference, Gray received a letter from outgoing Macmillan vice-president Robert Wilkie saying that Gage was "winding down what is left of the old Macmillan and disposing of all remaining stock by remaindering." (Gibson would recall later that, in fact, only the poorly selling Macmillan backlist titles were remaindered: "The ones that were continuing to sell were certainly kept in print. That goes on in every publishing house, whether they've been taken over or not.") The hardcover versions of four of Gray's titles—*The Winter Years*, *The Boy from Winnipeg*, *Red Lights on the Prairies*, and *The Roar of the Twenties*—were already out of print by 1981, and the last ninety-nine hardcover copies of *Troublemaker!* were being set aside for Gray should he wish to purchase them. "I regret this necessity," wrote Wilkie. "We are pleased to have been your publishers and have valued our association with you." Gray replied that he would be making arrangements with another publisher, Jack Stoddart of General Publishing, to have his out-of-print titles reprinted in paperback. Thus ended his fifteen-year relationship with Macmillan, the company with which he had achieved his greatest successes as an author.

Boomtime
1978-1980

While *Troublemaker!* marked the end of James H. Gray's fruitful six-book association with Macmillan, it did not mark the end of his career as an author. The journalists had now stopped believing him whenever he said he was going into "literary retirement," and so it came as no surprise to them in 1979 when they heard he was coming out with a book about the populating of the Prairies between the 1870s and the First World War. "I guess I am hopelessly addicted to book writing by now, a bookaholic as it were," Gray told *Albertan* columnist Eva Reid in a November 1979 interview shortly after he addressed Alberta Theatre Projects' annual Bob Edwards fundraising luncheon in Calgary.

Gray's new book was to be published by Western Producer Prairie Books, the Saskatoon-based company that Gray had accused of "botching" the publication of *Men Against the Desert* in 1967. Western Producer Books manager Rob Sanders—a former English teacher and sales representative for the Holt, Rinehart & Winston publishing company—had remained in touch with Gray over the years and, in 1978, finally convinced him that a "significant and new title by James H. Gray" should be published in 1980 to mark the joint seventy-fifth birthdays of the provinces of Alberta and Saskatchewan.

Gray happily agreed to do the anniversary book because it was not going to involve much in the way of research. He had already done the work during the early part of 1976 for a commissioned seven-thousand-word *Reader's Digest* article about prairie settlement that never appeared in the magazine. Doing the anniversary book would be simply a matter of reworking and expanding on what he had already written, adding photographic illustrations, and turning it into a social history text for use in high schools. Sanders read the unpublished magazine manuscript and decided that what had been a problem for *Reader's Digest* would not be a problem for Western Producer. *Digest* editor Hugh Durnford had said that the Gray piece would not work for the magazine because it failed to focus on "real people" and on personal experiences that were "heroic, funny or tragic." Gray had retorted in a letter to Durnford that such an approach would drastically oversimplify the story of one million immigrants flooding into a previously empty wilderness over the course of four decades. Durnford then asked one of the magazine's copy editors to rewrite the article with particular emphasis on the "everyday heroes" of the prairie settlement era. When that failed, Durnford spiked the article in May 1976 and paid Gray a kill fee of $250—one-quarter of the originally contracted amount.

Sanders told Gray that Western Producer would publish the material first as a trade book for commercial sale and later in a classroom edition. Gray sat down at his typewriter and four months later he turned in a manuscript of sixteen thousand words—more than twice the length of the original article. Using as his starting point the efforts made by the John A. Macdonald administration to lure British settlers to Canada during the 1870s, Gray went on to describe the aggressive immigration policy directed by the federal interior minister, Clifford Sifton, during the 1890s. He also wrote about the significant but little-known surge of immigration from the United States that he had talked about in his keynote address to the Destiny Canada conference in June 1977. Additionally, he wrote chapters about homesteading, prairie women, urban life, the ghettoization of eastern European settlers, and the evolution of modern prairie society.

Sanders asked Candace Sherk Savage—a twenty-nine-year-old editor and future writer of best-selling books on wildlife and cultural history—to edit the manuscript. Gray was so pleased with the way Savage reorganized the chapters to improve the flow of the text, and with the captions she wrote for the photographs, that he dedicated the book to her and offered to give her 40 percent of the royalties. "I don't know if it's fair or justified, but I do know that I feel very pleased about it," responded Savage. "You are a generous-minded man, and I thank you very much." She would recall later that after this experience of "playing hand-maiden to a great ego" she gave some thought to asking Gray if he would become her mentor. "He existed in my imagination as the person whose door I wanted to knock on. I was trying to become a writer myself and didn't really know what you did after you got up in the morning. He was one of the first people I met who was really doing it; who was getting up every morning and actually working as a writer. He knew a lot of things about being a professional writer that I really wanted to know, but I never did quite get up the courage to ask him."

Gray was also pleased with the title Savage suggested for the book: *Boomtime: Peopling the Canadian Prairies*. He was not pleased, however, when he viewed the galley proofs. Once again, Western Producer Prairie Books succeeded only in rankling him with what he saw as shoddy production values. "I am astounded beyond words at the book design," he wrote in a letter to Sanders in April 1979. "Any half-drunk apprentice printer could have produced a book that would at least feel like a book. They seem to be determined to cram the maximum amount of type onto every page and to use the least possible space for the pictures. Some are in fact reduced to silly sizes. The result is that it will establish a record as the thinnest coffee table book ever printed." Sanders took the criticism to heart. In May 1979, he told Gray that the book was being redesigned to increase the size of the photographs and leave more white space around the text: "The overall effect of this process will be to eliminate the cramped appearance of the pages and thus expand the book to approximately 140 pages."

While *Boomtime* kept him busy with revisions and editing, and *Troublemaker!* kept him busy with media interviews, Gray still managed to find time to continue with his ongoing crusade to have more Canadian history taught in schools across the Prairies. He donated medals and prize money to the universities in Calgary, Edmonton, Saskatoon, Regina, and Brandon to encourage students to excel in the study of western Canadian history. He also battled the educational bureaucracies in each of the prairie provinces over what he called "the interdiction of the teaching of history in the public schools." He had to be careful when he did this, however, because his son, Alan, and Alan's wife, Arlene, were both public school teachers in Calgary, and Gray did not want "a suspicion to arise in the administration that either of them are behind my agitations." Alan and Arlene had decided, however, that the most prudent course of action for them was to give Gray his head and not get involved. "He was going about it the wrong way," Alan would recall afterwards. "He had no teaching experience, so he really didn't know how the curriculum was put together or how it was taught." Arlene said it was embarrassing for them when Gray began pressing his case with Jake Longmore, who was chief schools superintendent for the Calgary Board of Education. "He went over the heads of the people that he should have talked to first," she said. "If he had a problem with the curriculum, he should have been talking to teachers before he talked to the superintendent. But that wasn't his way. His way was to take the superintendent of schools to the Petroleum Club for lunch."

As it turned out, Peter Lougheed's Conservative government in Alberta had already been working quietly on an elaborate $8,387,000 plan to put more Canadian learning materials into the schools. In 1976, with oil and gas royalty revenues pouring into government coffers, the Conservatives had established the twenty-five-billion-dollar Alberta Heritage Savings Trust Fund as a "rainy day" investment plan for the future. Annual returns from the fund were being earmarked for such programs as debt repayment, medical research, and education. One such program was the Alberta Heritage Learning Resources Project, an innovative venture with three main objectives: to increase Canadian content in the language arts, social studies, and science curricula of Alberta schools; to provide an educational outlet for authors, illustrators, and editors from Alberta and other parts of Canada; and to use Alberta presses for the printing and publishing of textbooks.

In January 1978, Gray received a letter from the Alberta provincial education ministry inviting him to serve on a government advisory committee that would be selecting thirty-two titles by Alberta authors for reprinting and distribution, not only to public schools, but also to universities, public libraries, hospitals, seniors' homes, and penal institutions throughout the province. Gray was reluctant at first to accept the invitation. "My experience leads me to suspect nothing but the worst," he wrote in a letter to the other committee members, who included prominent Alberta historians Grant MacEwan and Hugh Dempsey. "Having already been involved in a number of abortive efforts to bring some Canadian history into the Prairie provinces' school systems, I am hardly enchanted by the prospect of going through any more futile exercises." However, he changed his mind when he discovered that one of the government representatives on the committee would be Ken McVey, his former editor at Macmillan who had joined Alberta Culture as a literary consultant in October 1977. In a letter to McVey on 27 January 1978, Gray wrote: "If the advisory committee is allowed to play a useful role in bringing the glories of Canadian and Prairie history to the attention of our children and their teachers, then there is no length to which I will not go."

Gray served on the advisory committee from 1978 until early 1979, helping to choose thirty English-language books, one French-language book, and one Ukrainian-language book for distribution across the province. From his own list of published titles, he offered *Men Against the Desert*, which he cheekily described as "not only my best book but probably one of the most important books ever written about Canada, and one of the best written." He also offered *The Roar of the Twenties*. Other titles chosen by the committee included W. O. Mitchell's *Who Has Seen the Wind*, Maria Campbell's *Halfbreed*, Robert Kroetsch's *The Words of My Roaring*, Rudy Wiebe's *The Scorched Wood People*, and Myrna Kostash's *All of Baba's Children*. Four thousand sets of books were made up and some of the distribution took place during National Book Week, 2-8 April 1979, when twenty Alberta authors, including Gray, toured the province promoting Alberta books. Gray was clearly happy with the way the project had gone. "I came to this project full of suspicion and gloom," he wrote in a letter to fellow committee member Al Mitchner on 8 March 1979. "But my entire experience with the project has been one of awakening pleasure with the competence of all the people involved, and with their dedication and unselfishness."

A few months after Gray completed his work on the committee, he finished proofreading and correcting the manuscript for *Boomtime*. The book was published in October 1979, both as a hardcover coffee-table book and a paperback. "If the public reacts to *Boomtime* the way the media people reacted, it will be a best-seller," Gray told Western Producer's Rob Sanders after a short publicity tour. "I have never seen the interviewers evoke the kind of interest and enthusiasm they showed in Toronto, Winnipeg and Edmonton."

Most of the critics also evoked enthusiasm for the book. Gordon Dodds wrote in *Quill and Quire* that Gray's prose was a "delight at any time" and recommended that readers give the book more than a second glance. Henry C. Klassen, writing in *Alberta History*, likewise recommended the book "for it admirably sums up a good deal of the social history of the Canadian Prairies." David Neufeld observed in *Saskatchewan History* that Gray seemed to have written his book for people who derived most of their entertainment from television "and I think it will have some success against it." However, Neufeld did criticize the author for trying to pack too much into too little space: "In less than a page of text, Gray describes pre-fabricated housing, the loneliness of Prairie women, and church housing." Another criticism came from W. J. C. Cherwinski, writing in the *Canadian Book Review Annual*, who accused Gray of ignoring the "deep-rooted ethnic and social tensions and suspicions" that existed in the prairie provinces before the First World War, and of dwelling too much "in the world of the anecdotal, rose-coloured past."

In 1980, Gray was chosen by *Alberta Report* magazine as one of the top twelve Albertans of the 1970s "for creating a series of popular histories on the agonies and triumphs that brought about Western Canada." (Others on the list included Edmonton Oilers owner Peter Pocklington; Citadel Theatre founder Joe Shoctor; Premier Peter Lougheed; Progressive Conservative leader Joe Clark; and Dome Petroleum chairman Jack Gallagher.) Another honour came Gray's way in 1980 when *Boomtime* won Alberta Culture's one-thousand-dollar award for nonfiction. "It was an outstanding winner, I can tell you," said John Patrick Gillese, director of the literary arts branch of Alberta Culture. "It was a unanimous winner." Gillese added that the purpose of the award was to "draw attention to Alberta authors and to show them we're aware of the fine job they're doing."

Sanders predicted the attendant publicity would give sales of the book a boost. However, *Boomtime* did not become the success that he and Gray had hoped for. It sold fewer than five thousand copies and by September 1980—less than a year after publication—Western Producer had declared the hardcover edition out of print. Gray decided that poor distribution was the problem and told Sanders he would be offering his next book—about alcohol and its abuse after the repeal of Prohibition—to a larger publisher. Jack Stoddart of General Publishing had already expressed interest in publishing Gray's new writing, as well as keeping his old titles in print as paperbacks, and Gray was about to cut a deal with him. Or so he said.

Bacchanalia Revisited
1982

James H. Gray led Rob Sanders of Western Producer Prairie Books a merry dance while deciding who should publish what he called his "booze update"—an alarmist tract about the alcohol-related problems that followed the repeal of Prohibition in the 1920s. "The focus is broadening from a story concentrating on the Prairies to one that is national and, in a way, international in scope," Gray wrote in a letter to Sanders on 5 May 1981. "In that case, I have wondered whether you have the organization to handle it." Sanders quickly let Gray know that he was not about to give up the book without a struggle. "I am surprised by your letter indicating you are considering a larger publisher for the booze book," he wrote to Gray on 13 May 1981. "But I'm a grappler and I can't let go without a fight. It is too easy for many larger publishers to imply that only they can handle significant books and that smaller publishers lack the wherewithal to publish and sell books effectively in national or international markets."

The larger publisher, Jack Stoddart of General Publishing, had hardly done any original publishing up to that time. Like his father before him, Stoddart had made his money publishing paperback reprints of hardcover titles by successful Canadian authors, and by importing and distributing books by such internationally best-selling authors as Jacqueline Susann, Harold Robbins, and Carlos Castaneda. Stoddart had already made Gray happy by offering to reprint all of his remaindered Macmillan titles in softcover editions, and as a result Gray viewed Stoddart as the publisher who could give him the international exposure he desired.

It is doubtful, however, whether Gray ever seriously thought his booze treatise had international potential. It was quite limited in scope. The main focus was the extent to which alcohol abuse had contributed to crimes of violence and automobile accidents in western Canada from the 1920s onward. However, Gray did think it might strike a chord with Canadians in general. He recalled how in 1962 an American biologist named Rachel Carson had written a book called *Silent Spring*, which touched off a public debate about the use of poisonous chemicals to kill insects. He hoped his book would have a similar impact and cause Canadians to think and talk about alcohol-related problems.

On 7 October 1981, Stoddart wrote to Gray to say he would be reprinting *The Roar of the Twenties* as the first of Gray's Macmillan titles to appear as part of General Publishing's PaperJacks line. At the same time, he asked to see what Gray had done on the booze book "even if it is only partially written." Stoddart told Gray that General Publishing had editors on staff who would help him with the planning and shaping of his book "so that we as a publisher may contribute any input which might be helpful." By that time, however, Gray had already changed his mind about having Stoddart publish the book because he felt uneasy about the publisher's lack of experience with original man-uscripts. He wrote to Stoddart to say he was required by the option clause in his *Boomtime* contract to give Western Producer rights of first refusal on the manuscript. "It seemed to me," Gray told Sanders afterwards, "that citing the contract option was an easy way out of explaining why I was going to have you publish the book. In fact, the decision was strictly on a personal basis. I had talked to you about it before Stoddart came into the picture." Sanders said he had "no lack of enthusiasm" for the project and looked forward to seeing the finished manuscript.

Gray's in-basket was soon full as he compiled the research

material for what he called "a terribly difficult update of my *Booze* book." Aside from the various alcoholism studies, crime statistics, and liquor commission reports he had collected for the book, he also had letters relating to the history essay contests he was sponsoring in the schools; invitations to do speaking engagements; and a request from the Calgary Exhibition and Stampede for assistance in compiling a history of the Stampede. Gray said yes to most of these requests. "I really ought to get my head read for letting myself get talked into so many things at seventy-five years of age," he told his daughter Pat. But if a request gave him an opportunity to further the cause of history, he was always happy to comply. In a speech given at the seventieth anniversary dinner of the Calgary Public Library in January 1982, Gray said he first became addicted to social history during the 1930s, when he read the descriptions of nineteenth-century working conditions given by Karl Marx in *Das Kapital*, Marx's three-volume exposition of socialist theory. "I didn't know it at the time, but social history is what it was."

Yet, no matter how full his in-basket was, Gray always found time to go for a morning swim at the downtown YMCA, have a chicken sandwich and a game of gin rummy in the mahogany-panelled card room of the Petroleum Club, or attend the regular sessions of the Knights of the Round Table, a discussion group that met weekly in a hotel banquet room to listen to—and frequently badger—a sometimes-controversial lunchtime speaker. Gray was in typically testy form at a meeting of the Knights in September 1981, when the speaker was Reverend Lloyd C. Greenway, the twenty-seven-year-old pastor of Calgary's Metropolitan Community Church, one of seven churches in Canada that endorsed the homosexual lifestyle. During the question period, Gray stood up and asked Greenway, "Do you sodomize?" Jaws dropped, elbows nudged, and eyes rolled. "I'm a Calgarian," replied the flustered preacher, "not a Sodomite."

"Wait a minute, Mr. Greenway," said Gray. "Hold the phone there a minute. You haven't answered the question I just asked.

Do you do buggery?"

The chairman of the speakers' committee, Ed Wolf, looked pleadingly at the meeting chairman, William Downton, but Downton refused to rule Gray's questions out of order. Greenway was left to squirm like a worm on a hook. A week later, Wolf submitted his resignation from the Knights. He accused Gray of conducting a witch hunt and said his questioning was offensive. "Open exchange is one thing, but we don't pillory people," said Wolf. "We wouldn't ask a woman about her personal sexual practices, so why would we ask a man?"

When a member of the Knights leaked the story to *Alberta Report* magazine, Gray refused comment. "The Knights is a private club, and I don't think that anything that happened there is anybody's business but our own," he said. (In fact, the Knights had always welcomed media coverage of their meetings; Gray was just being his usual contrarian self.) Maureen Bell, one of the first women to join the Knights after its men-only membership restriction was lifted in 1975, defended the decision to allow Gray's questioning. Ruling it out of order would have been a form of censorship, she said, and contrary to the Knights' charter. "Guests are warned the questions can be tough," she added. "We are not known for our kindness."

Longtime Knights member Herb Allard would observe later that while Gray's line of questioning might have seemed provocative and confrontational at the time, he was only demonstrating that he was a product of a less enlightened, less tolerant era in Canadian social history. Gray had grown up during a period when homosexuality was outlawed in Canada and he was disturbed by the thought that a young pastor would now be sanctioning a lifestyle where consenting adults engaged in what he still regarded as "indecent acts." "Jim represented a generation that still viewed vagrancy as a crime and sodomy as a crime," said Allard. "He had a traditional view of the world that reflected the times. That's why he could be confrontational, asking challenging questions."

Asking challenging questions also defined Gray's approach to the problems of alcoholism as he worked on the manuscript of the book he would title *Bacchanalia Revisited: Western Canada's Boozy Skid to Social Disaster*. His questions were many: Why did prairie society allow boozing on the streets to become so widespread during the early 1980s that police in cities and towns across the West had to regularly employ water cannons to keep order? When would the citizens of the West stand up and demand an end to growing public alcoholism and violence? Would any prairie government take the lead and declare a moratorium on the issue of liquor licences for new cocktail bars and beer parlours? Would any government boost the price of beverage alcohol to a point where consumption might noticeably decrease?

The first part of *Bacchanalia* was essentially a recap of what Gray had already covered in such books as *Booze* and *The Roar of the Twenties*. He reiterated that the people of the Prairies had voted overwhelmingly for Prohibition in 1915 and 1916, and that it had brought a vast range of social benefits including less crime and fewer cases of spousal and child abuse. Then came the reintroduction of legal alcohol sales and the social problems started to mount again. With popular opinion swinging toward moderation rather than abstention, booze eventually became a "health-destructive, life-shortening threat to our society." To prove his point, Gray paraded a disturbing array of statistics throughout the book:

• Between 1935 and 1975, the population of the Prairies increased by 50 percent, while the number of alcoholics rose by 700 percent.

• Canadian deaths from cirrhosis of the liver rose from 64.34 deaths per million adults in 1935 to 107.99 deaths per million in 1956.

• In the first twenty years of the cocktail bar era—roughly

from 1958 to 1978—liquor consumption across the Prairies increased five-fold. Crime statistics kept pace.

• Of the 149,524 reported crimes of violence committed across Canada in 1978, between 30 and 51 percent were alcohol-related.

• Fifty percent of Canadian divorces granted on grounds of physical and mental cruelty in 1978 were considered alcohol-related. One-third of battered Canadian children in the same year were thought to be victims of alcohol-related abuse.

• In Alberta, more than twenty-five thousand motorists lost their licences annually because of drunk driving.

And so on. Gray was so shocked by the numbers that he gave up drinking hard liquor for a while. "I've never had a drinking problem," he told columnist Patrick Tivy of the *Calgary Herald*. "I've only been drunk twice in my life, when I had a couple of drinks too many. But I was so affected by what I was learning that I cut myself down. I haven't had a drink in two months." (He had, in fact, only stopped drinking rye and water—his favourite cocktail-hour beverage—but he still enjoyed a glass of German white wine at dinner.)

Along with the statistics, Gray offered the history of alcohol consumption in western Canada: By the mid-1920s, Prohibition was no more. The leaders of the temperance movement had grown tired or died or moved on. Governments had moved from liquor control to liquor marketing as they became increasingly dependent on profits from alcohol sales. Canadians discovered the charms of American-style bars and restaurants. Membership in Alcoholics Anonymous grew rapidly across the Prairies. Drinking to get drunk became common on Native reserves "because there was nothing else to do." The term "fetal alcohol syndrome" entered the language of elementary school teachers and social workers.

In his book, Gray proposed a series of drastic solutions to the problems he had uncovered. He suggested that governments should raise the drinking age; eliminate the advertising of alcohol on television; reduce the number of liquor outlets; dilute the alcoholic content of hard liquor, wine, and beer; increase the severity of sentences for criminal offences committed while drunk; and increase liquor prices to the point where a twenty-six-ounce bottle of whisky would cost sixty dollars and a case of twelve beer would sell for fifty dollars.

He stopped short of criticizing the politicians for granting tax breaks to distillers and brewers, and for turning the so-called liquor "control" boards into profitable marketing agencies, because he did not want his book to be viewed as a polemical tract against drinking. But that's how some in the media interpreted it anyhow. "James Gray is a bit surprised to find himself a social crusader in his old age," wrote Nancy Millar in the *Calgary Herald*. "But the research he uncovered during the writing of this book turned him into an active opponent of present-day attitudes and laws concerning liquor."

Bacchanalia Revisited was published in October 1982, and the reviews were generally favourable. Once again, Gray earned praise for writing about what Robert A. Campbell of North Vancouver's Capilano College described as "an almost untouched subject in Canadian social history." Ian L. Hepher wrote in the *Lethbridge Herald* that *Bacchanalia* was "an authoritative work on a contemporary social problem," and T. D. Regehr wrote in the *Canadian Historical Review* that the book "may well become a catalyst which challenges and reverses some contemporary public attitudes." However, the reviews also left the impression there was more misery than mirth in Gray's moralizing treatise, and this undoubtedly turned off potential buyers. After six months in the bookstores, *Bacchanalia* had sold fewer than two thousand copies, making it by far the least successful of his books.

Rob Sanders, who moved to Vancouver in 1987 to join Douglas & McIntyre as its trade-list publisher and eventually found its Greystone Books imprint, would recall later that even though the manuscript for *Bacchanalia* was not quite what he had expected when he agreed to contract terms with Gray ("I thought it would be more like *Booze* or *Red Lights on the Prairies*), he never gave any thought to stopping publication. "This was Jim Gray, after all," he said. "I really liked Jim. I felt very privileged to have known him and to have worked with him, so there's no way we would have backed down from publishing that." Gray did not mind that *Bacchanalia* was a relative failure. He had delivered his sermon and was already moving on to his next literary project—a history of the Calgary Exhibition and Stampede.

Cowboys and Counsels
1982-1986

Writing a history of the Calgary Stampede was the last thing James H. Gray had on his mind in January 1982, when he bashed out a nine-page memo in response to a request from the Stampede historical committee for advice on how best to commemorate the history of the one-hundred-year-old rodeo event that had transformed itself from a modest agricultural fair into the self-proclaimed "greatest outdoor show on Earth." Gray told the committee that the history of the Stampede should be chronicled "as part of and a reflection of the social history of southern Alberta," and that each chapter should cover the events of one decade, starting in 1884, when a group of Calgary citizens first got together to organize a fair. Gray offered the committee the following specific suggestions for writing the history:

> The book should be written with the maximum possible dispatch. Book writing is a world of its own, and the best books are those written in a white heat. My suggestion for your book would be: No more than a year between the commencement of writing and the delivery of the first draft of the completed manuscript. I would suggest the writer spend the first month reading and boning up on Alberta history. A second month could concentrate on the history of

the Stampede itself. In short, get the stuff into the writer's head. Then it ought to be possible to complete a chapter a month. When writing projects are allowed to drag, you lose track of what you have written. That is because when you get to chapter ten, two years have passed since you wrote chapter one. You repeat yourself over and over, discover on rereading that you have used and reused modes of expression, and have actually dealt with the same subject in two or three different places. Building a book is like building a house. If the process is not carried through quickly, far too much work has to be redone. Take the word of someone who learned the hard way! If the procedures and the time frame are fixed in the beginning, the house will get built. So will the book.

After reading Gray's memo, the committee members decided they should look no further for the person to write their book. Gray, if available, was clearly the best choice. They extended the invitation and Gray accepted. In an unrelated transaction, he also accepted an invitation from the Calgary Bar Association to write a history of the law in southern Alberta, based on a series of one-on-one interviews conducted by researcher Susie Sparks with senior bar members. Taking on two major writing projects at once was no problem for Gray at this stage. Writing books had been the principal focus of his life for twenty years and he had long accepted the fact that, despite his occasional claims to the contrary, he really did not want to spend his time doing anything else. His health was good, his mind was sharp, and there were still lots of stories to be told.

The Stampede story was long overdue. Twenty years previously, a Stampede publicist and former newsman named Fred Kennedy had written a short, ninety-six-page history of the annual western shindig that the event's first organizer—cowboy showman Guy Weadick—had predicted in 1912 would "make Buffalo Bill's

Wild West extravaganza look like a carnival sideshow." While Kennedy had uncovered a few of the Stampede's skeletons—including the fact that Weadick sued the board successfully for wrongful dismissal after being fired in 1932—he shone very little light into the darker corners of Stampede history, and left largely unexamined the impact of the event on Calgary's social, economic, and political life. Gray hoped to conduct a deeper investigation; spotlight the Stampede's escalating series of what he called "ever more absurd dreams and schemes"; and take a hard look at such issues as the mistreatment of rodeo animals and the fight waged by residents of Calgary's rundown Victoria Park neighbourhood to stop the Stampede from expanding into their front yards. However, because he was hired by the Stampede board to write the history, and because he had the Stampede historical committee looking over his shoulder as he wrote, it was perhaps inevitable that what Gray eventually produced would ruffle no Stampede feathers and please such corporate Stampede sponsors as Coca Cola, Imasco, Revelstoke, and Burns Meats—whose names he mentioned prominently in the text. Gray wrote the book under contract with the Stampede for ten thousand dollars, and also cut a side deal with the publisher—Western Producer Prairie Books—to receive a 5 percent royalty on all trade sales. With annual Stampede attendance running at around one million people, Gray hoped that many of the visitors would want to buy the book as a thirty-dollar souvenir.

While Gray was in the midst of researching and writing the Stampede book, he received a phone call from Brian Felesky, president of the Calgary Bar Association, asking if he would be interested in writing a book based on the oral history interviews Sparks had conducted with local lawyers and judges. Gray said he would write two sample chapters for one thousand dollars apiece and, if those were acceptable to the bar association executive, he would complete the book under a fee-plus-royalties arrangement similar to the one he had with the Stampede board. "Not only was I willing to become involved with the Bar Association project, I was downright eager to get on with it once the Stampede book was off to the publisher," he would write later in the introduction to the book he titled *Talk to My Lawyer!: Great Stories of Southern Alberta's Bar & Bench.* Meanwhile, he had come across several juicy stories of scandal, murder, and political intrigue while combing the back issues of the Calgary newspapers for Stampede material, and he was keen to put the best of them into a book.

With his unerring eye for a good anecdote, Gray found lots of colourful material in the newspaper archives to make the Stampede book, *A Brand of its Own: The 100 Year History of the Calgary Exhibition and Stampede,* one of his characteristic good reads. His finds included the following gems:

• When the Prince of Wales invited the Stampede rodeo champions to his southern Alberta ranch in 1923, he intended to present each with an engraved sterling silver cigarette case. However, bronc rider Pete Vandermeer came close to ruining what was supposed to be a routine photo opportunity when he refused to accept the royal gift. "Sorry, Prince," he explained, "but I don't smoke." Guy Weadick quickly saved the day by drawing the embarrassed prince to one side and whispering: "Tell him we'll get him a gold watch instead."

• The legend of rodeo cowboys riding their horses through hotel lobbies during Stampede week had its roots in a 1924 photo shoot staged by a *Calgary Herald* photographer who asked a rodeo contestant named Eddie Keen to pose on his pony in the doorway of a Stephen Avenue café as if he had just ridden through the premises.

• The popular tradition of serving pancakes on the street to Stampede visitors began in 1925, when a chuckwagon driver named Jack Morton parked his rig downtown after an impromptu wagon parade, fired up his cookstove, and began dispensing flapjacks to the gathering crowd.

• An ill-considered decision by the "try-anything-once" Stampede committee to join forces with the Calgary Winter Carnival to stage a ski jumping contest down a temporary slide connected to the roof of the Stampede grandstand resulted in a lot of red faces—not to mention a lot of expense—when a seasonal chinook in January 1921 melted all the snow on the slide and the event had to be cancelled.

Along with anecdotal material, Gray discovered a number of facts about the early days of the Stampede that contradicted claims being made by the publicity people in their promotional campaigns in 1982. The publicists were saying, for example, that the first Stampede in September 1912 was a "roaring success," whereas in reality, Gray found out it was an "unmixed disaster," due to poor planning, lengthy program delays, and rainy weather. The publicists also described the first Stampede as the "brainchild" of cowboy Guy Weadick, whereas the actual credit was due to H. C. Mc-Mullen, the Calgary livestock agent for the Canadian Pacific Railway, who saw how popular one-day rodeos were in small towns of southern Alberta and thought that a week-long rodeo in Calgary would be a major draw.

While Gray was completing work on the Stampede book, in the summer of 1985, he received a letter from the Calgary Board of Education (CBE) saying that only 211 students had submitted entries that year for the history essay contest he was sponsoring to the tune of $1,500 annually. Gray was not impressed. He had started the contest five years earlier with the hope that junior and senior high school students might be encouraged to use the materials he had helped put in the schools as part of the Alberta Heritage Learning Resources Project. Now the board was telling him that out of more than fifty thousand eligible entrants, less than 1 percent had applied. "This contest is flying with all the grace and style of a lead balloon," Gray commented. He cancelled the contest and spelled out his reasons in a letter to CBE trustees chairman Jon Havelock:

> Two generations of Calgary schoolteachers have gone through the system from kindergarten to B.Ed. degrees without ever having been forced to learn the salient facts of Canadian and Alberta history. So how can a profession whose knowledge intake has been so severely restricted be expected to evoke an interest in a contest on a western Canadian history theme? Obviously it could not. What we now have in Alberta is an educational system manned by Albertans who, in fifteen years of immersion in our system, have never been exposed to at least two dozen climactic events in Alberta, Prairie and Canadian history.

Havelock replied that the teachers hired by the CBE were well qualified to teach the social studies curriculum, which covered geography, as well as history, and included such history-related subjects as the development of Canada as a nation, industrialization in Canada, and human rights in Canada. However, Gray's mind was made up. He had decided—with some justification—that the education system's emphasis on Canadian and Alberta history was much lighter than the emphasis placed on language arts, science, and mathematics, and so he just decided to write off the contest as "another noble experiment that didn't work out." Instead, he would concentrate on doing what he did best—writing history books for people who wanted to know about their heritage.

It took Gray a year longer than he had anticipated to complete work on the Stampede book. The Stampede people had done a poor job of preserving their own history, and so Gray had to spend many weeks scrolling through public records to flesh out the material he had obtained from annual reports and board minutes. He also had to spend many weeks in the archives of Calgary's Glenbow Museum selecting photographs to effectively illustrate the text. When the book finally appeared in November 1985, it contained enough glossy pictures to justify the coffee-table designation and the thirty-dollar price tag.

Most of the reviews were positive. John Howse, writing in *Canadian Geographic*, praised Gray for effectively capturing the Stampede's colour, politics, and "the forces that drive its boast— unCanadian as it might seem—to be the Greatest Outdoor Show on Earth." Frank Moher wrote in *Alberta Report* magazine that "Mr. Gray can still ride a sentence out of the chute better than any of his competition." Max Foran, writing in *Alberta History*, described the book as "well-written, interesting and sound histor- ically." However, one media report annoyed Gray so much that he threatened to sue the publication, the *Calgary Herald*, and the writer, columnist Patrick Tivy, for libel.

Tivy had written that Gray "was hired by the Stampede board to tell their story . . . yet, despite his remarkable access to the Stampede's records, Gray spends little time examining the show's shadowy side." Gray bristled at the suggestion that he had been "financially influenced in the selection of materials by an inferred answerability to the Stampede board" and instructed his Calgary lawyer, Patricia Daunais, to advise the *Herald* that he considered the comments a "malicious libel." The threatened lawsuit quickly evap- orated, however, when *Herald* publisher J. Patrick O'Callaghan perused a limited edition of *A Brand of its Own,* published for Stampede board members and their corporate friends, and noticed that the foreword contained an acknowledgement of the help Gray had received from members of the Stampede historical committee. O'Callaghan pointed this out in a letter to Daunais, and Gray responded immediately by dropping his complaint. Instead he set- tled for having a letter printed in the *Herald* saying he had retained exclusive control over the writing of the manuscript, and that nobody on the board had ever sought to influence him.

The net effect of Gray's spat with the *Herald* was that he was unable to get needed publicity for the book during the period leading up to the Stampede of July 1986. When Fraser Seely, sales supervisor for Western Producer Prairie Books, inquired about the possibility of having a feature story or excerpts from the book run in the *Herald*, he was told by managing editor Kevin Peterson that the newspaper would not be doing anything further with the book because of the problems resulting from the Tivy column. Sales of the book suffered accordingly. During the first six months after its release, only 1,084 copies moved off the shelves.

A Brand of its Own was Gray's last book with Western Producer Prairie Books. Manager Rob Sanders decided after reading a draft of Gray's manuscript for *Talk to My Lawyer!* in January 1986 that the scope of the book was just too narrow. He told Gray that while the manuscript contained a number of fascinating and important stories—including the chronicling of a sex scandal that brought down Alberta Premier John Brownlee in 1933, and an account of the murder of an Alberta police officer that resulted in a Crowsnest Pass bootlegger named Emilio Picariello and his female accomplice going to the gallows in 1923—it had limited commercial sales potential outside of southern Alberta. Sanders said he would be interested in considering publication of a book about "the most fascinating and intriguing aspects of western Canadian social history as they relate specifically to legal matters." He added that he would also be interested in discussing the possibilities of a book covering the entire province of Alberta. But he was not interested in publishing the manuscript as written. Nor, when Gray told him that the lawyers might underwrite the cost of producing the book, was he interested in doing the book as a vanity publication for the Calgary Bar Association. "Any good printing company could do that, and the Bar Association should contact printers directly."

Before approaching the printing companies, Gray decided he would try Edmonton publisher Mel Hurtig to see if he might be interested in publishing the manuscript. Hurtig replied on 19

February 1986 that while there was "some great stuff and some terrific writing" in the book—he particularly liked the Brownlee sex scandal chapter and a chapter about the breakup of the law partnership of Sir James Lougheed and R. B. Bennett that gave rise to Bennett's career in federal politics—he, too, had trouble seeing the commercial viability of the book. Like Sanders, he suggested the book might work better if it covered northern as well as southern Alberta. But even then he could not see doing a print run of more than five thousand copies. Hurtig became more enthusiastic about the project when Gray told him that the lawyers had money to support the publication. On 21 May 1986, Hurtig wrote to Sparks to say his company would print five thousand copies of the book in return for a twenty-thousand-dollar subsidy guaranteed by the bar association. Hurtig Publishers would look after the editing, design, distribution, and advertising of the book, and it would be published in September 1987.

Gray enjoyed working on *Talk to My Lawyer!* The Brownlee case gave him an opportunity to titillate a modern readership with the sensational allegations of a twenty-one-year-old government stenographer who testified she "had connection" with the premier in a bedroom that he shared with his son while his ailing wife slept in a nearby bedroom. And the R. B. Bennett research allowed him to take a closer look at a prime minister often seen as the villain of the Great Depression. It also provided Gray with some of the raw material he would use for his next and final book—a full-length biography of this bachelor politician, who was once described by a political rival, Liberal Charles "Chubby" Power, as "exhibiting the manners of a Chicago policeman and the temperament of a Hollywood actor."

But while his working life continued to invigorate him, Gray's home life was now starting to become stressful. Kay's personality had changed—her short-term memory was failing and she lived in a constant state of anger and depression. Gray began to fear she might be suffering from a serious mental disorder. In July 1986, he made an appointment to see Dr. Keith Pearce, head of psychiatry at the University of Calgary. Gray duped Kay into accompanying him by saying that as they were both getting older they should now have a regular "mental check-up" in addition to their annual physical exam. Pearce referred them to Dr. Stephen Edwards, a specialist in psychology, and he offered the opinion that Kay's memory lapses and personality changes might signify the onset of dementia.

The Bennett Project
1986-1991

When *Talk to My Lawyer!* was published in September 1987, James H. Gray was already deeply immersed in what would be the last major literary project of his life—a biography of the man he viewed as "the greatest of our prime ministers and the most interesting." He had mentioned to several people—including University of Toronto history professor Michael Bliss—that he thought a biography of Richard Bedford Bennett would be worth doing because the politician had the worst reputation of any prime minister in history and "deserved redemption." However, Gray did not necessarily see this as something he would take on by himself ("an approaching octogenarian is hardly the one to tackle so daunting a project") and so he was pleased when Bliss put him in touch with a Halifax history professor, Peter Waite of Dalhousie University, who was already contemplating a biography of Bennett. Gray suggested that a collaboration might be in order.

Waite, an established biographer with well-received books on Prime Ministers Sir John A. Macdonald and Sir John Thompson to his credit, welcomed Gray's proposal that they work together. "There are real possibilities in our combining efforts," he said. "I don't know the Calgary ground." They agreed that Waite would cover the story of Bennett's early years in New Brunswick and the later period when he was prime minister, while Gray would cover the thirty years Bennett spent in Calgary before leaving for Ottawa to assume the leadership of the federal Conservative party. Gray started work on his part of the joint venture in the fall of 1986 while doing the final revisions and edits on the manuscript of *Talk to My Lawyer!* He received a grant of $21,078 from the Alberta Foundation for the Literary Arts to fund his research and writing, and that allowed him to spend time in Ottawa examining the microfilms of the Bennett papers at the National Archives of Canada. Waite, for his part, was still busy at Dalhousie, but expected to have more time to devote to Bennett after he retired from active teaching in April 1988.

By April 1987, the industrious Gray had put more than thirty thousand words about Bennett on paper. Waite reviewed the draft manuscript and suggested that Gray consider moving ahead on his own to do a popular biography of Bennett based on what he had already written. Doug Gibson had left Macmillan in early 1986 to begin a small select trade list at McClelland & Stewart under the Douglas Gibson Books imprint, and he had written to Gray saying he was keen to continue Macmillan's "grand tradition of publishing fine Canadian history—including Jimmie Gray's own books." (Gibson would recall later that he stayed in touch with Gray because he was interested in knowing how the aging author was faring: "I liked him a lot. He was always a breath of fresh western air in the Macmillan offices. He had one of the greatest grins in the western world.") Waite suggested that Gray should avail himself of the opportunity to publish with Gibson: "I don't want to give you up if I can help it, but I should be a little dismayed to think that I might be preventing you from turning your experience and knowledge of Bennett to some financial advantage." Gray replied that he still wanted to maintain the collaboration, though he was somewhat dismayed when sixty-five-year-old Waite said he wanted to spend a couple of years working on his part of the project to ensure it had "good underpinnings" and was sound academically. "You can write quite casually that you expect to work on Bennett 'for the next couple of years,'" said Gray. "I have to pummel myself to think in terms of beyond next Christmas! I am to be eighty-one years old this year."

As well as being concerned about his advancing age, Gray was also concerned about Kay's deteriorating health. In September 1987, he wrote to Waite to say that a diagnosis of Alzheimer's disease had been confirmed:

Kay has simply forgotten how to cook, and her short-term memory is seriously flawed. Most of the time, life goes on as normal, except that we go out to eat a lot more. But once every couple of months there is an aberrant episode—she gets mad at some triviality, takes the dog, calls a cab and goes to a friend's home on the other side of town, arriving in a somewhat incoherent state. Then the mood passes and everything reverts to normal for a month or so.

Learning to cope with this, learning to live with Alzheimer's disease, and keeping my concentration on the job at hand has been very difficult. Alzheimer's is a terribly insidious thing. It is only when something outrageously aberrant occurs and triggers a diagnosis that you realize it has been there for perhaps two years. But as my doctor says, it is probably the best way to die if freedom from pain is the sole criteria.

Ultimately institutionalizing must be faced, and I hope that is still a couple of years away. But it is very soon going to inhibit my ability to go on research safaris out of town.

In the midst of his private sadness surrounding Kay's illness came a moment of public celebration for Gray in 1987 when he received the Alberta Order of Excellence—the province's highest honour—for his pioneering work as a chronicler of western Canada's social history, and for his steadfast efforts to make history more prominent in the Alberta schools' curricula. "I feel like the luckiest Canadian in the world," he told an *Edmonton Journal* reporter. "This is the best surprise of my life."

On 20 December 1987, Gray wrote to Waite to say he had decided there was enough material on Bennett to make for a two-volume biography. "Moreover, it is a natural two-volume biography. The first will deal with his New Brunswick boyhood, his education and life as a lawyer and politician in Calgary up to his election as leader of the Conservative party. The second will finish him off."

Waite, however, was not keen on the two-volume idea: "They really are a nuisance to work with. I tend to regard them as a resort to be used only when we find out that what we've got to say can't be contained in one." Waite said that if Oxford historian A. J. P. Taylor could keep his 1972 biography of Lord Beaverbrook to one volume ("admittedly more than seven hundred pages"), then Waite and Gray should be able to do the same with their Bennett book. "And perhaps we ought to try. Marketing a two-volume work is more than a nuisance, it's an imposition."

In May 1988, Gray received word that he was to be appointed to the Order of Canada for his work as a social historian. He had been nominated, without his knowledge, by his son-in-law Bill Fennell, a semi-retired Kelowna accountant and Rotary district governor whom Pat had married in 1987 after her divorce from Bill Whittaker. Gray told a *Calgary Herald* reporter that the national recognition came as a bit of an anticlimax to him after the Alberta award of the previous year. "The first one is always the big one," he said. "But don't get me wrong. I'm absolutely thrilled about this one too."

Waite retired from Dalhousie University in September 1988. However, instead of taking the opportunity to now spend more time working with Gray on the Bennett project, he first took a temporary position with the history department at the University of Western Ontario and later accepted a commission from Dalhousie to write the official history of the university. That meant putting off his Bennett work for at least another two years.

By October 1988, Kay's health had deteriorated to the point where she could no longer look after herself at home. After talking it over with his son, Alan, Gray made the painful decision to have Kay move into a seniors' lodge run by the Metropolitan Calgary Foundation, where she would have a large private room and her meals prepared. Gray planned to visit her daily and bring her ice cream cones, her favourite treat. "It is a terribly wrenching experience, to find myself alone after sixty years of marriage," he wrote in a letter to Waite. He told his daughter-in-law, Arlene, that he particularly missed the "noisy quiet" associated with having another person in the house. His daughter Pat told him he should have a dog to keep him company, and so she drove him to Lacombe, Alberta, where a family friend had a one-year-old wire-haired terrier to give away. The terrier, named Jennifer, became a cherished household companion for Gray during the years that followed.

In December 1988, Gray suffered a minor heart attack. After a week in the hospital, he spent four days "holed up in the Palliser Hotel living off room service" and then wrote to Waite:

I am now into my eighty-third year and time is of the essence. My heart attack has very sharply focussed my attention on the fact that I am living on borrowed time and that unless I get with it, I may not be able to complete the Bennett project. Your letter saying that for the next two years your immediate concern must be with Dalhousie had the effect of a fire alarm going off. If it should happen that you might be forced to abandon the Bennett project entirely, perhaps what I have done might be published as a partial biography by my family.

Waite wrote back to assure Gray he had no intention of abandoning the Bennett project. "It's now so deep in my being that I can't give it up." He planned to work on the Bennett book "in bits and pieces" as his Dalhousie schedule would permit, and he wanted it to be "a credit not only to your vivacity, western experience and financial legerdemain, but also to whatever academic virtue and style I may be able to bring to bear." He added, however, that if Gray was impatient, he could always forge ahead with his own Bennett book.

Gray was indeed impatient. In a letter of reply, he wrote:

> You are sixty-six and I am pushing eighty-three. I can hardly remember when I was sixty-six. That was six books ago, for God's sake! I can remember how easily things came to me then, how easily I wrote then, and how uneasily I write today. The minor heart attack has certainly concentrated my mind wonderfully. This will, of course, be the last book I ever write, and I would like to see it at least partly off the press before I get lugged off to the marble orchard.

In October 1989, Gray received word from the Metropolitan Calgary Foundation that it could no longer take care of Kay's needs at the Jacques Lodge, and that she would have to be moved to a nursing home. "The process is brutal," Gray wrote in a letter to Waite on 27 October 1989. "It involves more medical examinations, court processes and God knows what. But, thank goodness, the light is now visible at the end of the tunnel. It has been a very wearing time for me, but the Bennett project has given me an ever-present escape hatch." Gray recalled that when he started working on the Bennett project, he was in a writing environment that he had enjoyed for twenty years, sharing a home with Kay and having her look after his domestic needs. But Kay's illness had shattered that environment:

> I now rattle around alone in an eight-roomed house. Kay's deteriorating condition has reached a point where she does

not remember in the afternoon a phone call that was made in the morning. Her condition is never far from my mind, and the Bennett project has become something increasingly difficult to cope with. But it's also something that provides a measure of meaning to existence. It is a sort of life preserver that I hold onto.

Waite repeated his suggestion that Gray might consider taking what he had already researched and written, and go to a publisher with it:

You could, in fact, do a book on Bennett's Calgary years quite on your own. But I think it would be a much better book if we could have input into all of it together. I suppose I am conservative, but I fear rushing into print with a half-baked piece of work. Working up the academic underpinnings, I would need time for that. I couldn't put my name to something that I don't find myself comfortable with.

Gray bristled at the suggestion that his research might be found wanting, but Waite hastened to assure him that his comments were not meant to cast aspersions on Gray's qualifications as a researcher, or on the quality of his writing:

I would just like our text and our footnotes to show that we have canvassed all the primary sources and the secondary literature. The academic community has been thirsting for a good work on Bennett for a number of years, so I would want it to be solid. One need not spell out the detail, but one does have to be aware of it.

On 18 November 1989, Gray wrote to say he could no longer wait for Waite to become actively involved in the Bennett project. He proposed the following:

I will take over the research and write the New Brunswick prelude to the Calgary years. I will then submit the manuscript to you for your decision as to whether you will agree to publication of this part of the project under our joint authorship. If your name is on the jacket, then you will share in the royalties. If, however, you decide you do not want your name on the first book, then the royalties will be mine.

Waite replied, without waiting to see the manuscript, that he would not want to put his name on something that was—apart from some material on Bennett's early years in New Brunswick—largely Gray's work. "Besides, there's my perennial academic hang-up: What have we missed?"

That marked the end of their collaboration. "I regret to have our joint project end this way, because I do so enjoy and profit from my association with you," Gray wrote. "But I have been regretfully forced to the conclusion that it would be foolhardy for me to ignore the calendar." While the partnership ended, the friendship endured. Gray continued to correspond with Waite during 1990, sometimes to give him an update on the progress of the Bennett book, and occasionally to write about his minor health setbacks. In October 1990, Gray suffered a series of so-called little strokes (transient ischemic attacks or TIAs) and ended up in the hospital for four days. "There is nothing like lying around in a brain scanner at the age of eighty-four to solidify your life priorities," he wrote in a letter to Waite on 17 October 1990. He added that the TIAs seemed to have impaired his short-term memory and also affected his ability to type.

Gray finished his Bennett manuscript in November 1990 and sent it off to McClelland & Stewart's Doug Gibson, who said he did not think it was "an M&S kind of book." (Gibson would explain later that Bennett by then had become just a "minor historical figure in the minds of the Canadian book-buying public. It was a case of the narrowness of the market, and not in any way a comment on the quality of the work that Jimmie had done.") But Gibson did think the manuscript might appeal to the editors at University of Toronto Press, and he offered to put Gray in touch with them. They reviewed the manuscript and quickly agreed to publish it—with the proviso that "rigorous editing" would be involved. So on 30 January 1991, in his eighty-fifth year, Gray signed a contract with U of T Press to complete a 110,000-word biography that would be titled *R. B. Bennett: The Calgary Years*.

Final Years
1991-1998

As well as being his last book, *R. B. Bennett: The Calgary Years* was James H. Gray's last hurrah as an historian. *R. B. Bennett* was a critically acclaimed biography that showed—as University of Toronto history professor Michael Bliss noted in *The Beaver* magazine—that Gray could write exhaustively researched scholarly history with the best of them. After being maligned for much of his book-writing career by academic critics who referred to him dismissively as a pop historian, at the end of the day Gray was praised by the academics for producing a biography that made an important contribution to the annals of Canadian politics.

Bennett had been an elusive target. Gray had found it almost impossible to reveal anything of the inner life of his subject because there were no personal diaries or private correspondence for him to consult. Bennett had burned all of his mother's letters to him and most of his correspondence with his alcoholic brother George and younger sister Mildred. His protective private secretary, Alice Millar, had shredded all of the papers she considered to be "without historic value." These included several exchanges of letters between the bachelor politician and various women with whom he was smitten. Nevertheless, Gray did manage to produce what Toronto historian Jack Granatstein called "the best look at Bennett so far."

The book was published on 26 October 1991. It had a print run of three thousand copies and sold for $29.95 a copy in hard-cover. Two months earlier, Gray had turned eighty-five, driven by himself to Winnipeg to visit with friends, come home, parked his old Mercury Cougar in the back alley, given the keys to his son, Alan, and turned in his driver's licence. His eyesight was failing because of macular degeneration, and he thought he should make the decision to quit driving before the licensing authorities made it for him.

The most laudatory of the academic reviews for the Bennett book—by U of T's Bliss and by Stuart R. Givens of Ohio's Bowling Green State University—praised Gray for successfully overcoming the difficulties posed by the fact that the Bennett papers fell silent at critical moments. The more lukewarm reviews, by the likes of John Herd Thompson of North Carolina's Duke University and Rae Murphy of Conestoga College in Kitchener, Ontario, said the book contained significant gaps but still managed to give some sense of how Bennett's life, until 1930, set the stage for his turbulent prime ministership. As for the reviews in the mainstream media, Peter C. Newman perhaps summed them up best when he announced in *Maclean's* magazine that he planned to give the book to a Calgary friend for Christmas. "I love all of Jim Gray's writing," wrote Newman. "He is the best regional writer in the country."

With the publication of Gray's book came the expressed hope from some reviewers that Peter Waite's promised second install-ment of the biography would soon be forthcoming. Waite, how-ever, had a different working method and was not about to jump into print before he was ready. "Jim was a reporter, used to getting things out in print once a modicum of research was in hand," Waite would recall in November 2004, when he was still some distance away from completing his long-awaited manuscript. "I, on the other hand, was and am an academic, wanting a decent mastery of the subject before getting it into print." With more than 627,000 documents, photographs, and other Bennett-related items housed in the archives of the University of New Brunswick in Fredericton, Waite, in 2004, still had some more sifting to do before offering his work for publication.

Gray's failing eyesight meant that even if he had wanted to take on another writing project after the Bennett book, it would have been physically impossible for him to do so. For a while he was able to read and type with the aid of an illuminated magnifier clamped to his desk, but a bout with shingles in 1994 robbed him of all but his peripheral vision, and that meant adjusting to a life without reading or writing. While he was angry and frustrated about this, he did not express his feelings publicly. "I've made peace with my limitations," he said in an interview with editor Jane Gurski for the foreword of a book about Bethany Lifeline, a medical alarm service that Gray subscribed to on the recommendation of his doctor. "In a way I'm lost, but I just cannot understand bitterness. I don't see how a person who's been as fortunate as I have been can be at all resentful about losing my sight. I can't rail against the fate that has overtaken me."

Privately, however, Gray resented the fact he could no longer read his morning newspaper to find out what was going on in the world, and was no longer able to do the daily crossword puzzle to keep his brain active. Instead, he now turned to television's *MacNeil/Lehrer Newshour* for the news of the day, and contented himself with answering questions from *Jeopardy!*—the popular American TV quiz show—to keep his mind busy. Whenever he talked about his eyesight problem to friends and family members, he invariably directed a stream of verbal abuse at the medical profession because it could not provide a cure for macular degeneration. He remained constantly frustrated and angry about his condition until he finally agreed with son, Alan, that he should start carrying a white cane. At that point, Gray became the surprised beneficiary of the kindness of strangers, who helped him across the street and pointed him in the right direction whenever he lost his bearings downtown.

Kay died on 5 August 1994, at age ninety-one, in the long-term care ward at the Foothills Hospital in Calgary, where she had been moved after leaving the Jacques Lodge in 1992. She had been married to Jimmie for sixty-seven years and—as he wrote in the *Calgary Herald* death notice—it had been a marriage "during which she was the most loyal of fellow travellers through the worst of years and through the best of years." In some respects, their relationship had been like that of the unsophisticated Nora Barnacle and her literary genius husband, James Joyce. Gray would often complain to his daughter Pat that Kay never read any of his books, and that her lack of social skills prevented him from moving in the exclusive circles that he felt were his due as a successful journalist and author. But it was a relationship that endured because they had married for life. When Jimmie and Kay exchanged their vows at Winnipeg city hall on 28 December 1926, they had publicly proclaimed a lifelong commitment to one another that neither would ever break.

There was no funeral service for Kay. The family scattered her ashes along a footpath in a little park that the subdivision developers had left among the houses built on the Grays' old Grasmere Farm property during the late 1970s. Gray planted a tree in the park in Kay's memory, and under the tree he set a copy of *The Winter Years*—the book he had dedicated to her for being "so much part of the surviving." Gray had been fending for himself for six years at the time of Kay's death, and he continued to live independently for two more years after that. He never learned to cook— "He would burn water," quipped his son-in-law, Bill Fennell—and so Gray regularly rode the bus to the Westgate shopping centre to order a take-out meal from Kentucky Fried Chicken, or travelled to the Tony Roma's restaurant downtown for a meal of beans, coleslaw, french fries, and onion rings, washed down with glasses of his favourite Riesling. He also met regularly with his pals for lunch at the Petroleum Club, usually ordering a large sandwich and then taking half of it home to eat for supper.

All of Gray's first and most successful books—from *The Winter*

Years to *Booze*—were out of print by the mid-1990s. His first publishers, Macmillan and Western Producer Prairie Books, were no
longer in business, and it seemed that Gray's long run as the country's foremost popular chronicler of western Canadian history had
ended. But just when he might have been about to fade into
obscurity, along came a Saskatoon (later, Calgary) publisher—Fifth
House Ltd.—to bring him to public attention again. Fifth House
publisher Fraser Seely knew Gray's work well from having worked
as a sales supervisor at Western Producer Prairie Books when it
published such Gray titles as *Boomtime, Bacchanalia Revisited*, and *A
Brand of its Own*. In the spring of 1995, he introduced a Fifth House
reprint line that he named Western Canadian Classics, and he
picked two of Gray's titles—*Red Lights on the Prairies* and *Booze*—
to launch the series. "They had been out of print far too long," he
recalled later. "They begged for reissue."

Seely, who had been visiting Calgary regularly to—as he jok-
ingly put it—"sneak in the back door from Saskatoon, looking for
things to publish," wanted to reprint Gray's books because he felt
they still contained some of the best writing available about the
history of western Canada. "The material was very accessible—it
reached out to a general audience—and they were roaring good
stories. How can you go wrong with something like *Red Lights on
the Prairies* or *Booze*? They are immediately interesting just to hear
about them, and then they are so well done."

Gray was delighted to hear that someone wanted to reprint his
books. After a couple of lunches with Seely at the Petroleum
Club—once joined by University of Saskatchewan historian Bill
Waiser, who subsequently wrote new introductions for five of
Gray's reissued titles—the author agreed to contract terms. (Waiser
recalled later that it was quite touching to see Gray, then legally
blind, being greeted at the door of the Petroleum Club by old
friends who had not seen him in some years. "He was obviously much
appreciated.") Fifth House managing editor Charlene Dobmeier—
mindful of Gray's failing eyesight—ensured that the font size was

very large in all correspondence that she sent to the aging author, and the books were republished to appreciative reviews. "These reissues should find him a new audience," Michael Maunder wrote in *Alberta Report* magazine. "The stories he tells deserve to be known."

While Gray's visual impairment left him without the ability to do any new writing, he still accepted invitations to give speeches— always earning standing ovations for his stirring hymns to Canadian history—and he continued to be honoured for his work as a social historian. In 1995, he became the second recipient of the Pierre Berton Award "for distinguished achievements in popularizing Canadian history." Berton agreed to have his name attached to the five-thousand-dollar award, given by Canada's National History Society, when he was declared the first winner in 1994. Former Prime Minister Joe Clark, a fan of Gray's writing and a director of the society, presented the award to the author at a dinner at the Petroleum Club in October 1995. Berton said in a short letter to Gray that he could not think of a more deserving recipient. The University of Toronto's Michael Bliss, another society director, also thought Gray was a worthy winner. "I always ranked Jimmie, along with Pierre Berton, as popular historians who were worth reading," he would recall later. "Gray was a natural historian. He had an open-minded, common-sense approach to life that made for good history writing."

In September 1996, the City of Calgary gave Gray's name to the little park in northwest Calgary where he had planted a tree in Kay's memory. At first he was upset when he heard about this— because his family had quietly arranged the dedication through the city parks department and the charitable Calgary Foundation without his knowledge—but he agreed to accept the recognition graciously when they explained that they wanted it to be a surprise for him. "It is indeed a great honour," he told a *Calgary Herald* reporter. "But I would prefer it be called Grasmere." At that point Gray was ninety years old and becoming increasingly frail. After he injured himself at home, falling down the stairs while going to the basement to feed his dog, Jennifer, he agreed with his son, Alan, that he should move into a seniors' home. His daughter Pat moved back to Calgary from Kelowna with her husband Bill Fennell to help Alan take care of their father's needs as he adjusted to living first at the Westview Lodge and later at the Edgemont Retirement Residence, where he vented his frustrations daily by banging his white cane on the floor, much to the annoyance of the other residents. Gray's dog, Jennifer, was given to a family friend whose own wire-haired terrier had recently died.

Gray's last years were difficult. A stroke in the summer of 1997 put him in the Peter Lougheed hospital for several months until he could be moved to his final residence, the Bowview Manor nursing home. The stroke destroyed his memory. When an Edmonton historical researcher, Moira Calder, phoned him at the nursing home in the fall of 1998 to verify some information for a multivolume journalistic history series entitled *Alberta in the 20th Century*, Gray told her sadly that he could not remember most of the people he had once known and had also forgotten about most of what he had written. During their telephone call, Gray asked Calder if she was a Christian. When she replied that she was, he said, "Well, that's the difference because I have nothing. I'm an atheist. I'm sick. I'm blind. I live within these four walls, and I'm waiting to die." He had told his doctor that if he became comatose, "I do not want to be given the benefit of any artificial or mechanical or electronic so-called life-support systems."

Gray died on 12 November 1998 at age ninety-two. "He was ready to go," recalled Pat. "He really had given up at that point." Describing himself as "a little bit of everyone I have ever met," Gray did not leave to chance the way he would be publicly remembered—his last piece of writing was his own death notice. "One of Canada's literary treasures," he wrote. "When such people pass away, so does a library of unpublished information, ideas and memories."

His ashes were scattered in the little Calgary park that bears his name. Obituaries were published in both of Canada's nationally distributed newspapers—*The Globe and Mail* and the *National Post*—and in regional dailies from Vancouver to Montreal. University of Saskatchewan historian Bill Waiser wrote in the *Globe*'s "Lives Lived" column that Gray's "keen sense of a good anecdote made him one of Western Canada's most successful social historians." Waiser observed later that Gray had been looking at social history topics for at least ten years before Canada's professional historians started doing the same: "He was pushing the profession in that direction even if he never got the credit for it." *Alberta Report* columnist Ted Byfield, writing in the *Post*, noted that Gray had left a vast cultural legacy: "He was unquestionably the best writer of history in western Canada that we ever produced. The whole of the Canadian West is the beneficiary." As if to echo that sentiment, the *Literary Review of Canada* in November 2005 chose *Red Lights on the Prairies* as one of the one hundred most important books in Canadian literary history. Gray's book was one of just three western Canadian titles to make the list; the other two were W. O. Mitchell's *Who Has Seen the Wind* and Rudy Wiebe's *The Temptations of Big Bear.*

Fifth House would continue to keep Gray's name before the public by reprinting his books. In 2005, the students at Calgary's Vincent Massey Junior High brought the author into the Internet age by creating a website showcasing his life and work. It came about at the behest of the Calgary Board of Education, which invited students to choose someone from their community to publicly honour during Alberta's centennial. The staff at Vincent Massey suggested that Gray be picked because of his contributions as a historian; because he had lived in nearby Strathcona Park; and because both his daughter Pat and daughter-in-law, Arlene, had worked at the school. (Pat worked as a secretary and Arlene as a teacher.) The students were not initially enthused about the idea, but they warmed to the task when they learned that Gray—far from being a dry-as-dust chronicler—was actually a salty-tongued character whom they admiringly described as being both "passionate" and "irascible." "His many classic volumes are still in print today and undoubtedly will be for a long time to come," wrote the students. "Long live the legacy of The Gray!" The author would have undoubtedly approved.

A Note on Sources

James H. Gray, for the most part, avoided putting footnotes or endnotes in his books because, as he said once in a letter to Toronto historian Ramsay Cook, he viewed himself as a popular historian not as a "frustrated academician, bemused by footnotes, who attacks archival material with a vacuum cleaner—sucking it in and spewing it out with total disregard for relevance." So in keeping with the Gray tradition I, too, have opted not to include footnotes or endnotes in this biography, for which I started collecting newspaper and magazine clippings after his death in November 1998. However, because the reader may be curious about my primary sources of information, here are some general notes:

Prologue: Canada's Highest Honour

James Gray's daughter Patricia Fennell wrote a detailed account of their trip to Ottawa for the Order of Canada ceremony—including such information as the colour of the carpeting in the Chateau Laurier's second-floor suites—in a letter to her parents that is now archived in the James H. Gray fonds in the University of Calgary's Special Collections department, on the twelfth floor of the MacKimmie Library Tower. She showed me the investiture program and banquet menu that she kept as souvenirs, and also described the event for me in an interview conducted for this biography on 12 July 2004.

Early Years—1906–1922

The general descriptions of early twentieth-century Winnipeg in this chapter are mainly drawn from such books as *Winnipeg: Heart of the Continent* by Christopher Dafoe (Great Plains Publications, 1998); *The Desire of Every Living Thing: A Search for Home* by Don Gillmor (Random House Canada, 1999); *A Winnipeg Album: Glimpses of the Way We Were* by John David Hamilton and Bonnie Dickie (Hounslow Press, 1998); *Winnipeg: An Illustrated History* by Alan Artibise (National Museums of Canada, 1977); and *Winnipeg: Where the New West Begins: An Illustrated History* by Eric Wells (Windsor Publications, 1982).

I also relied to a great extent on James Gray's own description of the Winnipeg of his boyhood in *The Boy from Winnipeg* (Macmillan of Canada, 1970, and Fifth House Ltd., 1996). Additional information came from a taped interview that Gray did with his son, Alan, in

August 1997. I obtained Gray genealogical data from the records of Ontario Vital Statistics and the Manitoba Vital Statistics Agency, as well as from the family history file of James Gray's cousin, Wayne Gray, which he was kind enough to lend me for this biography. Weather information came from the valuable historic data section of the Environment Canada website, which provides day-to-day data from weather stations across Canada dating back to 1840.

Down and Out in Winnipeg—
1930-1931

James Gray provided much of the autobiographical material for this chapter in such books as *The Boy from Winnipeg* and *The Winter Years* (Macmillan of Canada, 1966, and Fifth House Ltd., 2003, respectively). I obtained additional information from taped interviews Gray did with his son, Alan, and with Calgary literary historian George Melnyk. I appreciated having Calgary writer Shirlee Smith Matheson's transcript of the 24 June 1996 interview with Melnyk at hand when I wrote this chapter. I also appreciated the fact that Gray spoke about this part of his life during his fiftieth wedding anniversary celebration at the Calgary Petroleum Club in December 1976. A tape recording of that

event is archived in the University of Calgary's Special Collections department.

Reading and Writing—
1931–1934

James Gray offers a detailed description of his life on unemployment relief in *The Winter Years*. He described the beginnings of his career as a journalist in his 1996 interview with George Melnyk and in his book, *Troublemaker!: A Fighting Journalist's Personal Record of the Two Booming Decades that Followed The Winter Years* (Macmillan of Canada, 1978).

On to Ottawa—1935

The definitive book on the On-to-Ottawa Trek and Regina riot of 1935 is Bill Waiser's *All Hell Can't Stop Us* (Fifth House Ltd., 2003). Gray's account of his own role in covering the trek and its aftermath is detailed in his book *Troublemaker!* His correspondence with his cousin, Wayne Gray, is archived in the University of Calgary's Special Collections department. His daughter Patricia Fennell told me about the accidental deaths in the Burns family during an interview conducted for this biography on 2 August 2004.

Playing Oliver Twist—1937

James Gray gives a detailed account of the events described

in this chapter in his book *Troublemaker!*

Sitting Out the Second World War—1939–1945

Gray wrote about the events described in this chapter in his book *Troublemaker!* and he talked about them in a 1976 interview with Calgary historian David Bercuson. A transcript of that interview is archived in the University of Calgary's Special Collections department.

Ottawa Correspondent —1946-1947

The information in this chapter comes mainly from *Troublemaker!* and from Bruce Hutchison's autobiography, *The Far Side of the Street* (Macmillan of Canada, 1976).

A "Prairie Cassandra"—1947–1955

The information in this chapter comes mainly from *Troublemaker!* and from the Gray letters archived in the University of Calgary's Special Collections department. Additional information came from interviews I conducted for this biography between 2004 and 2006 with his children, Patricia Fennell, Alan Gray, and Linda Ostafichuk. I found Gray's editorials for the *Farm and Ranch Review* in the back issues of the magazine that are on file at the Glenbow Museum and Archives.

Adventures in the Oil Patch—1955–1964

Much of the information in this chapter comes from *Troublemaker!* and from Philip Smith's *The Treasure-Seekers: The Men Who Built Home Oil* (Macmillan of Canada, 1978).

The Winter Years—1962–1965

Gray described his efforts to get *The Winter Years* published in various newspaper stories that appeared after the book came out in 1966. Copies of these newspaper stories and the correspondence he exchanged with Macmillan are archived in the University of Calgary's Special Collections department. I found additional material for this chapter in the Macmillan Company of Canada fonds at the Morris Library at McMaster University in Hamilton, Ontario. I also found it interesting to read the various drafts of Gray's *Winter Years* manuscript as it evolved over the years.

A Prairie Historian Emerges—1966

All of the correspondence and copies of many of the reviews of Gray's books referred to in this chapter are archived in the University of Calgary's Special Collections department. I tracked down additional reviews using as my point of departure the biographical materials on Gray that are filed in the Local History Collection on the fourth floor of the Calgary Public Library's W. R. Castell Central Library.

Men Against the Desert—1965-1969

I found it both instructive and revealing to have a copy of *Men Against the Desert* (Western Producer Prairie Books, 1967, and Fifth House Ltd., 1996) at my right-hand side while reviewing Gray's exchange of correspondence first with Macmillan and then with Western Producer Prairie Books.

The Boy from Winnipeg—1969

The private exchanges of correspondence between Gray and Macmillan are in the University of Calgary's Special Collections department. The internal Macmillan memos, which provide an interesting background to the "official" communications, are in the Macmillan fonds at McMaster University.

Red Lights on the Prairies—1971

University of Toronto historian Michael Bliss elaborated on his initial response to the Gray manuscript for *Red Lights on the Prairies* (Macmillan of Canada, 1971, and Fifth House Ltd., 1995) in a phone interview I conducted with him for this biography on 9 February 2006.

Booze—1972

The story of the Bronfman family's initial displeasure with *Booze* (Macmillan of Canada, 1972, and Fifth House Ltd., 1995), which has never been told publicly before, is all detailed in the Gray correspondence files in the University of Calgary's Special Collections department.

Cracking the American Market—1973–1979

Aside from the material on The Writers' Union of Canada (TWUC) that I found in the Gray correspondence files, I also obtained valuable information on Gray's involvement with TWUC during the course of an interview I conducted with former TWUC chairman Andreas Schroeder for this biography on 7 June 2004. Additional insight came in a letter I received from the late Pierre Berton on 25 June 2004.

The Roar of the Twenties—1975

A copy of the speech Gray gave when receiving his honorary degree from the University of Manitoba is archived, along with copies of his other speeches, in the University of Calgary's

Special Collections department.

History in the Schools—1975-1977

Gray's daughter Pat told me about the 1944 trip with her father to New York in an interview I conducted with her for this biography on 12 July 2004. A tape recording of the fiftieth wedding anniversary celebration, archived in the University of Calgary's Special Collections department, gave me everything I needed to tell the story of that happy event.

Selling the Farm—1977

All the material on the 1977 Destiny Canada conference is contained in the Gray papers archived in the University of Calgary's Special Collections department. Information about the sale of Grasmere Farm is also in the Gray papers.

Troublemaker!—1977-1978

Much of the information for this chapter came from the Gray papers archived in the University of Calgary's Special Collections department. Additional information about the publication of *Troublemaker!* and the sale of Macmillan to Gage came from McClelland & Stewart's Doug Gibson during the course of an interview I conducted with him for this biography on 1 February 2006.

Boomtime—1978–1980

Saskatoon writer Candace Savage told me about her experience working as an editor on *Boomtime: Peopling the Canadian Prairies* (Western Producer Prairie Books, 1979) in an interview conducted for this biography on 20 February 2006. Gray's son, Alan, and his wife, Arlene, both retired educators, provided additional information about the author's crusade to have more history taught in Canadian schools during the course of interviews I conducted with them for this biography in March 2005.

Bacchanalia Revisted—1982

Rob Sanders, now publisher of Greystone Books, elaborated on his dealings with Gray prior to the publication of *Bacchanalia Revisited: Western Canada's Boozy Skid to Social Disaster* (Western Producer Prairie Books, 1982) in an interview I conducted with him for this biography on 10 February 2006. Information about Gray's social life and eating and drinking habits was provided in an interview with his daughter Patricia and her husband, Bill Fennell. I obtained additional information on the Knights of the Round Table incident through interviews I conducted with Knights members Frank Byrne and Herb Allard in February 2006.

Cowboys And Counsels—
1982–1986

Former *Calgary Herald* columnist Patrick Tivy elaborated on Gray's threatened lawsuit against the newspaper over Tivy's review of *A Brand of its Own: The 100 Year History of the Calgary Exhibition and Stampede* (Western Producer Prairie Books, 1985) in an exchange of e-mail correspondence with me in June 2004. Gray wrote about his wife Kay's memory lapses and personality changes in letters to his children that are archived in the University of Calgary's Special Collections department.

The Bennett Project—
1986–1991

The lively exchange of correspondence between Gray and Peter Waite is archived in the University of Calgary's Special Collections department. Doug Gibson elaborated on the reasons McClelland & Stewart turned down the Bennett manuscript in an interview I conducted with him for this biography on 1 February 2006.

Final Years—1991–1998

Much of the information about Gray's deteriorating eyesight and declining health came from interviews I conducted with his daughter Patricia and her husband, Bill Fennell, for this biog-

raphy. Former Fifth House publisher Fraser Seely told me in an interview on 21 March 2005 about his decision to have Gray's books reprinted. Edmonton historical researcher Moira Calder told me about her phone conversation with Gray shortly before his death. Gray's daughter-in-law, Arlene Gray, and the students at Vincent Massey Junior High school in Calgary told me about the James H. Gray website project found at http://tinyurl.com/c8r65.

Acknowledgements

James H. Gray always knew he could count on librarians and archivists to help him while researching his books. By way of thanks, he donated his manuscripts and correspondence to the Glenbow Museum and the University of Calgary, starting in the late 1970s. "Who knows what good they are?" he wrote in a letter to University of Toronto historian Michael Bliss on 18 November 1973. "But someone, some day, might get some use from them, along with what research material I have collected."

Count me as someone who got plenty of use from them. I am very grateful to Apollonia Steele and her staff in the Special Collections Library at the University of Calgary for all the assistance they provided to me during the many enjoyable months I spent going through the boxes of Gray's papers (stacked 7.4 metres high). I am also grateful to Gray himself for making life easy for a biographer by including a wealth of autobiographical material in such books as *The Winter Years*, *The Boy from Winnipeg*, and *Troublemaker!* Plus, he left behind a number of letters and taped interviews about his life and work, which more than compensate for his never having kept a personal diary.

I did not have an opportunity to conduct any interviews with Gray myself, but would like to thank those who did. They include University of Calgary historian David Bercuson, who did a series of taped interviews with Gray in May 1976; Calgary researcher Jane Gurski, who interviewed Gray in 1994 for a book about Bethany Lifeline subscribers called *Wisdom and Spirit*; Calgary literary historian George Melnyk, who conducted a lengthy taped interview in June 1996 that was transcribed by Shirlee Smith Matheson; and Gray's son, Alan, who did a taped interview for his family history about a year before his father's death in November 1998. I also want to thank Wayne Gray—James Gray's first cousin once removed—who entrusted his family history file to me so that I could match his genealogical research against the anecdotal, and not always entirely reliable, accounts in his cousin's books and letters.

I am grateful to many people who wrote or spoke to me about Gray and gave me other kinds of assistance when I looked for it. These include Herb Allard, Jim Bacque, Murray Ball, the late Pierre Berton, Michael Bliss, Bob Bott, Frank Byrne, Moira Calder, Hugh Dempsey, Charlene Dobmeier, Bill Freeman, Doug Gibson, John Martland, the late Pat Nagle, Harry M. Sanders, Rob Sanders, Candace Savage, Andreas Schroeder, Fraser Seely, Allan Shute, Don Smith, Glenn Sundstrom, Patrick Tivy, the late Reg Vickers, Bill Waiser, and Peter Waite. Finally, I would like to express my great appreciation for all the assistance provided by James Gray's daughter Pat and her husband, Bill Fennell; Gray's son, Alan, and his wife, Arlene; and Gray's daughter Linda in Fort St. John, British Columbia, who graciously answered my many questions and provided me with many valuable insights.

Index